THE SECRET LIVES OF GARDEN BIRDS

To Carolyn, my loving wife

 for birds
for people
for ever

The RSPB works for a healthy environment rich in birds and wildlife.
It depends on the support and generosity of others to make a difference. It works with bird and
habitat conservation organisations in a global partnership called BirdLife International.

If you would like to know more about the RSPB, visit the website at www.rspb.org or write to:
The RSPB, The Lodge, Sandy, Bedfordshire, SG19 2DL; telephone 01767 680551.

Photographers (by page number)

Chris Knights (RSPB Images): p138

Gordon Langsbury: pp40, 54, 76, 89, 90, 91, 94, 97, 101, 113, 131, 144, 149, 150

Hans Reinhard (Bruce Coleman): p88

David Tipling (Windrush Photos): pp6, 11, 12, 13, 18, 19, 27, 39, 46, 50, 53, 62, 64, 96, 124, 125, 126, 129, 133, 140, 148

The following photographs were all used with the kind permission of Windrush Photos:
Peter Cairns p10; Kevin Carlson p52; R. J. Chandler p151; Colin Carver pp24, 102; F. Desmete p82; Michael Gore p152;
J. Hollis pp45, 74, 104; Mick Ladner p133; J Lawton-Roberts p28; Tim Loseby pp115, 145; David Mason pp31, 108;
George McCarthy p30; Mike McKavett p47; Jari Peltomaki p130; Alan Petty p15; Roger Tidman p105;
David Tomlinson p92; Steve Young p79

Front cover: Wren on washing line (Jan Godwin, Still Pictures)

First published 2004, reprinted 2004, 2005 (twice) and 2006 by Christopher Helm,
an imprint of A & C Black Publishers Ltd., 38 Soho Square, London W1B 3HD

Copyright © 2004 text by Dominic Couzens
Copyright © 2004 illustrations by Peter Partington

The right of Dominic Couzens to be identified as the author of this work has been asserted
by him in accordance with the Copyright, Designs and Patents Act 1988

ISBN-10: 0-7136-6616-1
ISBN-13: 978-0-7136-6616-8

A CIP catalogue record for this book is available from the British Library.

A & C Black uses paper produced with elemental chlorine-free pulp, harvested from managed sustainable forests.

www.acblack.com

Typeset and designed by A & C Black, London

Printed and bound in Italy by G. Canale and C. S.p.a.

10 9 8 7 6 5

THE
SECRET LIVES OF
GARDEN BIRDS

Dominic Couzens
Illustrated by Peter Partington

Photographs by Gordon Langsbury,
David Tipling and Windrush Photos

CHRISTOPHER HELM
LONDON

Contents

Introduction

WE HUMANS ARE by nature curious creatures – that's curious in the investigative sense, you understand, although there are grounds for embracing the other meaning, too. We have always been so. Our curiosity stretches from our back gardens to the moon and beyond. If there are questions to ask, we ask them.

In recent years there has been a trend towards investigating the exotic and faraway. Programmes on television and radio have inspired us to travel, not just passively in our front rooms and imaginations, but actively too: to go there in person and see marvels for ourselves. If we're lucky enough to have such opportunities, of course we should take them.

But it would be sad if, in casting our eyes across the continents, we were to overlook the humdrum and close at hand. For in these familiar places there are also marvels to be seen and appreciated, and to enjoy these wonders is much simpler and less expensive than crossing to the other side of the world. If we are in search of mystery, there is still plenty of it outside our back door.

That's what this book is about. It's about the birds of the garden, birds that many of us meet every day. It's about characters that, because of their proximity to us, fool us into thinking that we know a lot about them. And yet we don't. If there was nothing new to find, the scientists wouldn't be making remarkable and eye-opening discoveries about garden birds every few months – the Starlings that leave roosts every three minutes, the Swallows that kill the infants, and the Dunnocks with their multiple partners. Not one of these behaviours was known about thirty years ago. And the more detailed the studies, the more fascinating and unexpected the lives of our garden birds turn out to be. The garden is truly a stage for shock, drama and intrigue.

The aim of this book, then, is to make you look at your familiar birds and be amazed at what they get up to. It's a book of gossip – although, hopefully, the kind backed up entirely by fact. My hope in writing this book is that we will all become curtain-twitchers of the birdwatching kind: those who watch their feathered visitors with an observing eye and let their curiosity take them where it will.

LOOK OUTSIDE and the newly crowned January garden gives few hints that a fresh year has begun. The grey skies and lifeless branches of interminable December remain in place, and the days are still grudgingly short, and the light is still pallid and apologetic. Even the frost covering the lawn on January 1st has effectively been donated from the year just past.

JANUARY

The Hidden Spring

IT MIGHT BE the beginning of a new year, but the birds don't seem to have noticed. They bustle to and fro from the feeders and bicker with each other, in just the same way as they have been doing for months, their minds grimly preoccupied with bare survival. Each day is a struggle, just like the last.

But something has changed, something very important. The days, short as they are, are no longer diminishing in length, but have just begun getting longer, and this turnaround is a significant biological trigger. It is no less than the starting gun for the breeding season to come, setting the birds off on their first lap of a marathon that will eventually lead to them producing eggs and young. Right now, even among the lifelessness of a cold and weary garden, comes a huge reawakening of breeding activity, spawned by this most reliable of natural indicators.

Nothing much shows at first, despite the Big

Switch. That's because most of the activity is internal. Light-detecting cells in the brains of birds have registered the change in day-length and already set in motion countless chemical reactions. Over the course of time many hormones are sent forth to prepare the birds' bodies for breeding. Little shows on the outside, but inside, from now on, the chemistry will be truly raging.

A Song for Spring

Although you cannot watch hormones buzzing around a bird's system, you can certainly detect small hints of their activity. It's like observing a person in love – they might not tell you much about it, but the odd comment or mannerism will soon betray their feelings. For birds, the most obvious sign that things are changing is song. Song is the coming together of bird notes to make phrases or sentences rather than monosyllabic calls, and is a certain prelude to breeding. Even by the end of December some birds start up on finer days, their apologetic notes gently caressing the damp, listless air. The two-note chime of the Great Tit, ever-cheerful and simple, strikes the future death of winter, whilst the Dunnock embarks upon what will be a complicated breeding season with a sweet and wistful warble. These, plus Wren, Robin, Blue Tit and Song Thrush are the lead vocalists, and many others will follow until, by the end of January, there is almost a chorus.

There may even be more visible signs of breeding. A Magpie, for example, might sneak a few sticks into a tree in dress-rehearsal for nest-building. Blue Tits might visit a nest-box as a couple and peck around the edges of the hole, as if measuring it up for future use. Such winter's day flirtations are almost always stimulated by a spell of mild weather, a secondary releaser to breeding behaviour now that day-length's bell has sounded.

In early January, then, comes the true dawn of spring: not in February, when the old saying

Left: Snow may be falling – but Great Tits are already gearing up for the breeding season.

Previous page: A snowy day's hard labour for a Coal Tit and a Goldcrest.

suggests that all birds should be paired by St Valentine's Day; nor in March, when the meteorologists decree it. The season starts now, strange as it may seem, during these seemingly unsuitable and dangerous times.

If birds had an opinion on such things, they would probably not be grateful for this extra burden. Midwinter is staring them in the face. Preparing for the future must seem like a dangerous luxury, as irrelevant to them as a pension plan is to a person facing starvation. A perverse combination of cold conditions and long dark nights in January means that virtually all of a bird's energies must be put into pure survival, nothing more and nothing less.

Life, in fact, is rather simple. A bird needs food, water and shelter, and if it gets these it has a reasonable chance of survival. If not, it will not last long. A very simple but deadly equation looms over every bird's life. If an individual can find enough food during the daylight hours to fuel it for the following night, it will live; if it doesn't it will starve before dawn. Birds are small animals, and have a high body temperature of about 40°C. To sustain this requires a lot of energy at the best of times, let alone during the gnawing chill of winter nights. Not surprisingly, bad weather in all its forms – cold, frost, snow, wind, even fog – squeezes the equation during the day by making food harder to find.

This puts enormous pressure on the hours when food is readily available. We are used to birds visiting our feeders with particular vigour and frequency during cold weather, but that is just a snapshot of reality. The amount of time

Refuelling is a full-time job for Blue Tits, even with a reliable food source.

that our garden birds, especially the smaller species, spend looking for food is scarcely believable. In the Great Tit, diminutive but not tiny, 75% of its waking hours are taken up with this task. The Blue Tit is occupied 85% of the time and the Coal Tit 90% of it. The smallest of our birds, the Goldcrest, spends literally all day feeding. Its days are a non-stop binge with no time to interact, no time to show curiosity, and with no time to rest. It might sound like one of the better Mediterranean cruises, but it's not an orgy of pleasure.

It is tempting to feel especially sorry for this smallest of birds; with its high surface-to-volume ratio, the Goldcrest is uniquely vulnerable to night-time cold. But there are advantages to being small. The Goldcrest lives in coniferous trees, where it can probe its ultra-thin bill among the densely-packed needles, looking for semi-microscopic insects. It has no real competitors in this mini-forest, and consequently not many distractions in the course of its frenetic days. The Goldcrest's habitat also ensures that it has "home insurance" against fierce weather. Needle-like foliage forms a barrier to any snow or hoar-frost cover that the winter may bring, so the Goldcrest has its own private, protected micro-habitat in which to search for food all day long. Although every bird faces the same struggle - to find enough food each day to survive – different species handle the search in different ways. Not all are fortunate like the Goldcrest in having a reliable, consistent supply of the same kind of stuff each day. Most others must shift from one type of food to another, depending on what is available.

Few are better at doing this than the Blackbird; it has a real gift for improvisation. It can turn bill and stomach to a whole range of foods, and its brain to acquiring them. Its regular diet is varied enough, with worms, smaller insects, spiders and fruit all common items on the menu. But wherever it lives it may add an assortment of extras, such as kitchen scraps, small fish, newts, frogs and even mice when needed. It doesn't mind getting its bill dirty either, poking around rubbish heaps and turning over cat and dog faeces. But perhaps the most remarkable example of the Blackbird's mettle in the face of hard weather was observed in the winter of 1975/76 in Devon. A certain Blackbird, finding its feeding area covered with some 2-5cm of snow, took a short stick in its bill and proceeded to flick the

powder away as one would use a brush. Having used its tool, it proceeded to forage over the cleared area. Now that's a survivor!

Hidden Talents

The Song Thrush feeds on much the same normal food as the Blackbird, and spends much of its life in competition with it. It's smaller than the Blackbird, and less adaptable. But it has one special talent that gives it an edge in times of trouble: of all garden birds, only it can break open the shells of snails, which it does by beating the shell against a hard surface with a quick sideways flick of the head. It's a time-consuming activity and draws unwelcome attention from predators and competitors alike, but snails are the Song Thrush's emergency ration, its own version of Kendal Mint Cake. If you must have just one major talent, it might as well be one that you can depend upon.

The Robin, for its part, has a special gift, too. Living its life mainly in the dark shade of damp woods and thickets, where it searches for the movements of small ground-dwelling insects, the Robin has large eyes for its size, and is good at working in low light intensities. This means that it can feed earlier and later in the day than most other birds and, in suburbia, it has adapted faster than most to foraging under artificial light. Robins have been seen catching flying insects at street lights and illuminated windows, especially in cold weather. They often sing in these alien conditions, too, lit by flashing neon signs and supermarket illuminations, embracing a modern 24-hour lifestyle more readily than many of us. Late night chorister Robins, singing in the winter gloaming, are often confused with Nightingales – but the latter are migrants, long gone and at present basking in African heat.

Not every bird adapts in a pleasing or laudable way to the rigours of food finding during winter cold. The freezing garden is a jungle, so to speak, with desperate violence never far away. Birds kill each other, by out-competing their peers, stealing from them, or consuming them directly. Carrion Crows, normally fierce rather than bloodthirsty, target smaller birds weakened by hunger, and both Magpies and Jays may follow suit. Herons, faced with frozen ponds, catch birds coming down to small puddles of free water. Female

The tiny needle-billed Goldcrest finds its insect prey in parts of plants other birds can't reach.

Hard midwinter frosts compound the problems birds face in their struggle to eat enough to survive.

Sparrowhawks, hungry beyond redemption, catch and kill the smaller males. These are bizarre acts brought about by naked need.

Of course January, in common with all months, does have its different moods. Its cruellest sulks result in the most deaths, putting too many obstacles in the way of birds' chances. A heavy snowfall, for example, whites out feeding sites as well as coming with bitter cold. Hard frosts are twin killers with frozen water. Wind and rain buffet birds and interfere with foraging. The longer these periods last, the more dangerous they are, and whatever some birds do, they simply cannot survive. In the worst winters, huge numbers of garden birds succumb.

An Early Start

January is not immune from more benign moods as well, though. In recent years we seem to have seen little snow and fewer frosts, and our birds have thrived accordingly. The days have been just as short, but their content has been gentler.

Whenever they have occurred, these quieter spells have always seen the occasional audacious breeding attempt by a small handful of garden bird species, especially those that are regular customers at well stocked bird tables. Blackbirds and Robins sometimes build nests and even lay eggs in January, although very seldom do these spawn surviving young. Pigeons and doves are much more regular and successful at midwinter child-rearing, since their internal chemistry is geared to continuous production throughout the year. Even in the wild, pigeons turn out young in a way that resembles a factory production line.

These instances remind us that the first month of the year is a double-edged sword. The change in day-length is irreversible, and so is the rush to breeding. Biologically birds have entered their so-called "acceleration phase," and accelerate they will, despite the hardships of the fickle January weather.

Winter, in its way, plays an important role in every bird's breeding season. The challenges it poses ensures that only the best survivors make it through the harsher months, those that have fought successfully against others of their kind, those that have avoided predation and those that have escaped the insidious cull of disease. January helps to sift out the weak, and leave the field to the fit.

After all this one would expect the survivors to face lessened pressures at the death of midwinter. But on the contrary, their problems are just beginning.

Robins and Spades

TO MANY PEOPLE the sight of a "friendly" Robin on a spade embodies the warm relationship that can develop between gardener and bird, a bond that finds its greatest expression when the trusting mite comes down to take mealworms out of the hand. People love Robins, and the birds reciprocate by being tame and endearing.

Of course there is no actual warmth on the Robins' side; they are not the slightest bit interested in us or our welfare. In normal circumstances, faced by our great bulk and greater capacity for causing trouble, they would run a mile. But we are useful, and can play a part in their survival.

For a start, a spade makes a good lookout post. Long before any human tools had been invented, Robins were drawn to perches at just the same height a few feet off the ground. With their keen eyesight they could scan the ground below for any insects that might scuttle across the forest floor, and then nip quickly down to grab them. Perch and pounce is their thing, and spades make good perches.

Fielding the Flushed

A Robin's ease with humans is harder to explain, but observations from the wildwoods can give us some insight as to why they approach so close to us when other birds fly away. In forests Robins have been seen on many occasions following deer, wild boar and other large animals about as they grazed or rooted among the trees. By disturbing the foliage and soil, the larger animals flushed out insects, giving a following Robin a supply of easy meals. On a smaller scale, entrepreneurial Robins also track tunnelling moles, fielding the small insects and worms as they flee their subterranean killer. The birds have even been known to snatch a juicy worm

virtually from out of a mole's jaws.

Now, if you will pardon the inference, it is a short step, at least in activity, from a wild boar to a gardener – rooting about, turning over the soil, disturbing insect cubby-holes. To a Robin, a working gardener is an opportunity.

The garden, in fact, is a Robin paradise. The tapestry of herbaceous growth, trees and open lawn is a reflection of its primeval habitat, giving it every chance to thrive. Our helpful activities are, if you like, the icing on the cake – or at least the wild boar on the forest floor.

Keeping up with the times: the Robin's ancestors only used branches for lookout posts and song-posts; now it's spades.

A View to a Kill – Sparrowhawk Strategies

IF SPARROWHAWKS WERE human, they would drive fast cars and live life hard. Theirs is a life full of daring, full of risk and recklessness. It has high rewards and heavy consequences.

Sparrowhawks are the garden's executioners. They feed on small birds and nothing else. Their lives depend on daily death, and each death is a high-speed chase. We might be appalled by what they do, but we cannot deny its drama.

Small birds, of course, are fast and mobile prey, and they do not intend to be caught. They take care of themselves. They rarely ever lose their guard. They come to the bird table, or to the ground, having checked carefully first; then they look up every few seconds, maintaining constant vigilance. They keep together in flocks, so that more pairs of eyes spot danger. When nervous they have alarm calls to alert each other. The small birds have solidarity.

The Sparrowhawk must break through all these barriers. Every day it must catch several birds. Otherwise it will starve.

Countdown to a Kill

The countdown to a strike begins in a hiding place, some distance from a potential meal. Sitting silently and still, usually in a tree, the Sparrowhawk watches the neighbourhood below it, looking for signs of bird movement. Quite naturally it has eyes like a hawk, specially adapted to pick out the smallest details, even those far away. As soon as a flock gathers on a garden lawn, or there is a burst of activity at the feeders, it will be alerted. If nothing happens for a while it will change perches and perspective, focusing upon a different set of potential targets a few hundred metres away. It pays to have plenty of shops in your local area.

Once a target has been selected, the Sparrowhawk makes final preparations. It will probably bob its head up and down a few times to judge distance, and then silently take flight. Keeping its quarry in sight, it lets gravity and a few flaps of its powerful wings accelerate it to a dizzying speed downwards towards a potential victim. In its final approach it

will level out, make one or two adjustments, and then plunge towards its prey.

Those last few seconds are unpredictable and dangerous. Rarely does a Sparrowhawk's target meet death in instant, peaceful ignorance, having never seen its killer coming. There is almost always a last second panic, flight and dodge. Birds have lightning reactions and the Sparrowhawk's main challenge is to snuff out any attempt to escape, however audacious. In these last moments it will follow its prey with complete abandon, utterly focused and beyond

Eyes of a hawk: it has the look of a crazed killer, but the Sparrowhawk is a planner and a strategist.

distraction, letting the victim go where it will, this way and that, until it comes within reach. Should the smaller bird have the slightest brush with the pin-sharp claws on a Sparrowhawk's talons, it will sustain mortal damage and the pursuit is over. But often the chase is well matched, running its sickening course in an aerial dance, then to the ground, even into the undergrowth on foot.

The final act of a chase is intended to be fatal for the quarry – perhaps one in ten strikes are successful – but for the Sparrowhawk it also carries considerable risk. With its sights set

15

unerringly on following a moving target, the hunter is looking through tunnel vision, with its surroundings blurred. It is, perhaps, equivalent to a cat-and-mouse chase on a human road, where the participants temporarily forget their safety and sanity in the intoxicating thrill of the pursuit. Sparrowhawks regularly come to grief by hitting obstacles, especially windows, and knocking themselves senseless. Many perish this way; others end up injured and die a slow death from starvation. Sparrowhawks have flown through open doors and become trapped inside rooms; others have been floored by colliding with human beings; others have struck overhead wires or cars during their high-speed chases.

But Sparrowhawks are not the maniacs of the bird world, they are the stuntmen. Much as they might let safety behind at the denouement of the strike, so they plan for a smooth operation before they start, and, figuratively at least, hope it works.

Top: *The Sparrowhawk slips down silently from a hidden perch, its first move towards a strike. If all goes well, its quarry won't see it coming until it's too late.*

Bottom: *Sparrowhawks have sharp beaks, but they catch their prey with their talons. It only takes the slightest brush to inflict a mortal wound.*

Behind the psychotic stare of a Sparrowhawk is a strategist and a master tactician.

There is evidence, for example, that these birds suss out their routes in advance; they don't go so far as to measure the speed and distance from departure to collision, like some kind of traffic policeman, but they do appear to fly along a potential course from time to time and learn the twists and turns. Sparrowhawks tend to live in certain areas for long periods, making this forward planning possible. It is likely that they acquire some kind of "map" in their brains of their home range.

The key to a successful capture is a concealed approach, and this will determine an individual's favourite striking sites. To be successful a Sparrowhawk seeks those places where small birds might be a little more vulnerable to unnoticed advance than they might be elsewhere. Open ground near cover is often ideal. In the countryside a regular tactic is to accelerate along one side of a hedgerow, then flip over the top and make a grab. In towns a Sparrowhawk will often come upon its prey from a neighbouring garden, keeping low and then looping over a fence. Any obstacle can be used for concealment: a tree, a house, a car, even the clothes upon a washing line. Go out into the garden to feed your birds and you might even find yourself used for an ambush, in an act of breathtaking impertinence.

Some Sparrowhawks are eerily cunning and versatile. There are reports of them flying alongside moving cars, using them as a mobile screen before accelerating over the bonnet and into an astonished flock of outwitted prey species. On other occasions they have been seen to take birds on the bounce as the latter have struck windows in an escape-flight panic: fast reactions, or was it the intention? They are regularly seen attacking birds temporarily cornered in squirrel-proof bird feeders with wire surrounds. Such feeders have not been around for long in the shops, but the hunters appear to have seized upon the opportunities they provide. These are all the acts of a sophisticated killer.

In many gardens, Sparrowhawks are not popular. Small birds, cute and vulnerable, lend themselves to favour at their executioner's expense. But it depends what we admire. If we respect stealth and cunning, and have a sneaking regard for speed and risk, perhaps we will set aside our bias and welcome the Sparrowhawk's fleeting incursions and serial liquidations into our gardens. If not, then perhaps that says something about us: we are unlikely ourselves to get into our cars and press the accelerator hard.

Battles on the Feeder

BLOOD IS SELDOM shed upon the bird table, but intimidation and food-stealing are just as deadly; it's just that their consequences are hidden from us. The starved corpse doesn't bleed.

A feeder is a place of conflict. By providing so much food, regularly and in concentrated amounts, we ourselves make sure of this, quite unintentionally, but inevitably. In midwinter, when food is otherwise scarce, and time is always short, the bird table can be a lifeline. In really serious conditions one can draw an unpalatable and uncomfortable analogy with the uncontrolled delivery of food parcels to starving humans. Those that are desperate are not democratic.

A Greenfinch shows its reluctance to share a feeder with a Great Tit. Even when food seems abundant, birds cannot afford to be complacent.

It doesn't take long to observe that every bird feeder encourages bullying. There are two forms of this, the simplest being a sharp peck towards a

rival aimed at driving it away; this is known in ethological parlance as a "supplanting attack". The other, slightly more refined form of bullying is robbery. A persecutor waits for its subordinate to obtain food from a feeder and then nicks its bounty, carrying out what we would call a mugging, with violence either threatened or used. Both forms are rife, even in the most genteel neighbourhoods.

Winners and Losers

It's often easy to detect the dominance relationships between different species. Blue Tits and Great Tits are pretty well matched, surprisingly considering the greater bulk of the latter – but Blue Tits are both irrepressible and irritable characters. Both of these species gleefully persecute the smaller and slighter Coal Tit, which does well if it can even spirit in to the bottom of a hanging feeder, take a nut and leg it without being challenged. All the tits cower when a Nuthatch arrives, hefty and armed with a long, sharp bill. But, in turn, the Nuthatch gives way to a Great Spotted Woodpecker.

And there are Greenfinches bullying House Sparrows, Starlings driving away Blackbirds, and pigeons making all the rest of the bird community scatter. Every garden watcher can make their own list, noting winners and losers, and cheering when an underdog prevails.

Hidden beneath these easily observed relationships are the subtler rankings formed between different individuals of the same species. They are no less prevalent than the between-species rivalries, and are often, in fact, far more important. In winter many birds spend time together in flocks: these include tits, finches, pigeons and Starlings. Hierarchies form within these groups. The odd scuffle on a feeder may be just part of a running battle that can last, in fits and starts, all day long, and beyond.

Battles on the feeder, then, are not petty or inconsequential; neither are they infrequent. In a flock in woodland (and so, we may conclude, something similar happens in the garden) scientists have found that a Great Tit is the victim of a supplanting attack on average five times every hour through the day. The average Blue Tit is harassed fifteen times every hour, and the poor,

hard-pressed Coal Tit twenty-three times an hour - once every three minutes or so. Almost all the Blue Tit and Great Tit skirmishes involved two members of the same species, but the Coal Tit is a frequent victim of the other two.

But however often they happen, skirmishes on the feeder always take up time and energy for the antagonists, all of which one would assume would be better spent actually finding food. But with not enough resources to please everybody all of the time, it pays to fight off a potential rival, time and again. If you're a loser, of course, you also expend energy, but without gaining a prize at the end of it, so your misfortune is multiplied. But conflict is essential to resolve these issues.

It is easy for us to watch the action at the bird table with fascination, even amusement. From the comfort of our living rooms, the bickering seems a small part of daily life. To the protagonists, though, it is deadly serious.

Who'd be a Heron?

IF YOU LIKE fish, you probably don't appreciate herons calling at your pond. But be sure of this: your visitors most certainly appreciate you! A reliably stocked pond can be a godsend to a heron in the midst of winter, just as a regularly stocked bird table can be a lifeline to an assortment of landbirds. If you think about it, there isn't much difference between one feeding station and the other; it's just that one's under water.

The conflict comes when the long-legged visitor outdoes its welcome and picks out a prized Koi Carp just acquired from the owner's latest visit to the garden centre. But who's to blame? Certainly not the heron; it's going for a rare easy option in a world full of difficult options. Away from the garden, its angling lifestyle is fraught with difficulty, and prone to frustration, wasted energy, and failure. Many herons cannot cope at all.

The main feeding technique of a heron looks simple enough. The bird wanders slowly along the edge of a river or pond, sometimes barely toe-paddling, sometimes immersing up to its belly, whichever technique enables it to overlook fish-rich water. Once settled at a suitable spot, it stands motionless, watching. If a fish comes within range the heron will lower its head and neck, little by little, smoothly and silently, crouching until the bill is close to the target. The final strike is quick, like the firing of a harpoon, the fish wriggles and is swallowed. The prey is never speared, but simply snatched, although the heavy, dagger-shaped bill might be called upon to administer some lunging, subduing stabs, as if emulating the scene in the shower-room of the Bates Motel in *Psycho*.

Against the Odds

All this, of course, is easier in the telling than in the doing. Fish are easily spooked; a false move may lead to many minutes of patience being wasted, the hunter going hungry. Fish are also maddeningly peripatetic; they come and go as they please, swimming back and forth. Their capture must seem like a lottery at times.

The odds are further lengthened by the problem of refraction, the change in angle of light entering the denser medium of water. It must seem extraordinary to a young beginner heron to

find that where it actually makes a strike is not necessarily where it thinks it is aiming. Older herons can be seen to compensate for refraction by moving their head and neck from side to side for a little while, carefully calculating the distance to the prey. But the mystery must be unfathomable to the apprentice angler.

Other problems affect the water surface, too. How often, for example, is water perfectly still, especially in winter? Lakes and ponds, even garden ones are often in draughty, open places, where the wind rustles up wavelets and turns a glassy surface into a glinting, impenetrable barrier. Rain must have the same sort of effect, too, stirring up the surface and making confusing patterns. And on good days the sun can reflect off the surface to pose another set of questions. Herons stand in the air and strike into the water, an occupation fraught with inherent difficulty.

These snags can be overcome, or at least ameliorated, by selecting a patch of water that is sheltered and calm. But finding such a place is like searching for a parking space in a town centre; there are not enough good sites to go around, and invariably someone else has got there first. No heron will share a good feeding site, and any incumbent will fight to keep it private when challenged.

One might have hoped that herons would be more inclined to share their resources when circumstances become desperate, but fishing is not really compatible with chummy sociability. Ask any human angler. What he needs is privacy, a place where no one will frighten the fish, interfere with his line or disturb his concentration. Herons need even more consideration. It simply will not do if a long period of patient waiting is interrupted at the last moment by a fellow fisherman wading idly past. For a hungry heron, such a disturbance could be the start of a long decline into weakness and, eventually, death.

Of all the hardships that herons suffer, though, none is quite as devastating as a long winter freeze. Ice not only places a glaze over the surface of the water, but also locks the hunter out physically, keeping the heron's food away under its hard

A heron resting beside a frozen pond. Sometimes all it can do is wait for a thaw.

surface. A heron facing a frozen pond is like a starving shopper arriving at a closed supermarket, made all the worse, perhaps, by what is desired being visible through the frosty glass.

Although some herons are adaptable and resort to finding unusual food in the winter chill, such as other birds or small mammals, many are forced simply to sit it out and wait for conditions to change. Then they are at the mercy of a cruel equation. On average a heron eats about a fifth of its body weight each day; it's not long before the numbers simply don't add up. Mortality can be as high as seventy percent in severe winters.

So spare a thought for your miscreant heron this January. You love your fish; of course you do. But so does the heron, and it needs them very badly. The best any heron could ever hope for this winter would be a well stocked pond in a garden with a sympathetic owner.

BIRDS MIGHT be a little reluctant to betray their spring-like feelings in the first month of the year, but in February all pretence is thrown off as birds sing, display and perform everywhere, whenever they can. The weather might still be vicious at times, and there will be plenty of cold spells when all exuberance is dampened, but overall the breeding season has been truly uncloaked; it is no longer a secret.

FEBRUARY

Take Your Partner(s)

BACK NEAR THE start of the year the change in day-length activated a switch, and it set our garden birds' hormones loose around their bodies with the brief to prepare their owners to breed. Just lately this internal chemistry has been having an increasing effect, not least upon the birds' reproductive organs. Birds are unique among higher animals in that these grow seasonally. Outside breeding they are deemed surplus to requirements, and shrivel almost to nothing. But in early spring the ovaries and testes enlarge by as much as a thousand times in a female and three hundred times in a male. This doesn't happen overnight, and the sexual organs become ready for different species and individuals at different times. Until they have been completely resurrected, of course, nobody can actually start producing fertile eggs.

But that does not stop the sexes taking notice of one another. February is a month for finding a mate, or for rekindling a previous attachment. It is also a season for taking up a territory – or house-hunting, if you'd rather. The mechanics of both are complicated, and vary greatly between species.

Coping with February fever is probably most comfortable for birds that stay together for life, or at least for season after season: these fortunate ones can focus their amorous reawakenings towards an already acquired mate. There are a surprising number of species like these in the garden. All our pigeons – Feral Pigeons, Woodpigeons and Collared Doves – form long-term pair bonds, and spend the warmer days of February cuddling close together on a high perch, such as a rooftop, preening each other like love-struck teenagers. House Sparrows, too, do not need to go looking. Their attachments are already formed, both to their mates and to their fellow colony

members; theirs will be a very sociable season. Birds as diverse as Tawny Owls, Nuthatches and Marsh Tits live private lives in a single territory, like self-contained stockbrokers, and have their pairing days far behind them. To them, the season approaches in unstrained togetherness.

There is a similar, but slightly less cosy type of relationship. This is the kind in which two birds that have spent the winter separately re-form their partnership from the previous season. These are marriages of convenience, one might say, conjured up from past history, proximity and familiarity. Such arrangements require rekindling work at the beginning, and some nourishment along the way, but they presumably cut out some of the stress of searching for someone completely new. Blackbirds can form these bonds and so, perhaps surprisingly, do many small short-lived birds such as tits, Robins and Chaffinches.

Still another form of relationship can blossom between birds that have got to know each other previously, but only recently - in winter flocks, for example. Tits and finches often form such bonds and one finch, the Siskin, has been known to form liaisons that span oceans and seas. Pairing up on their wintering grounds in Britain, "newlyweds" of these birds migrate over the North Sea together to Scandinavia to breed.

Finding a Mate

But of course, many birds enter the sharp end of the breeding season with sap rising but no mate. For them the next few weeks will be busy ones, full of advertising, assessing and readjusting. They must seek out unpaired members of the opposite sex, and decide whom to entrust with the important

Previous page: *February Fever: Collared Doves engaged in mutual preening.*

Left: *Two Woodpigeons developing a pair bond will spend hours tenderly preening each other.*

House Sparrows pair for life, so the early-season struggle to find a mate passes them serenely by.

task of propagating their genetic material. We know remarkably little about this aspect of a bird's life. We don't know how many different individuals of the opposite sex the average bachelor bird will meet and consider, and we don't know whether their experience is most like speed-dating or more protracted and courteous. We don't know, either, what exactly makes one bird favour another – well, we hardly know this for ourselves. We can only watch what birds do and speculate on their passions.

We do know for sure that song usually plays a role in selection. Song helps to space males out into territories and define them as individuals, and this enables females to form opinions about them, each on his home ground. It is inevitable too that, in the act of singing, a male will disclose honest information about himself, whether intentionally or not. His rate of output, or his repertoire, might tell a female enough to give him a miss, or to make a move. Song is the equivalent of a Lonely Hearts column in a newspaper: "I'm unpaired and seeking…" But unlike the human kind, a song is a true description of the singer, with no room for exaggerating qualities.

Singing will often be the initial link between a potential pair, like a human pair of eyes meeting across a room, but of course it cannot in itself seal the pair bond. The next step is a physical demonstration of some form, a courtship display.

Courtship displays are rituals signalling a bird's inner motivation, and they are standardised so that the potential mate understands exactly what the other bird is doing and why. When visited by a female, a male Chaffinch, for example, performs a fluttering, moth-like flight below her, beating his

25

wings rapidly to show off his bright white wing-bars. To keep her attention he then lands on a perch below her, crouches down upon it and tilts his body so that one side of him faces upwards, revealing the intoxicating sight of his belly. This so-called Crouching-lopsided display asks a definite question of a female, quite unambiguously. It's up to her to come up with an answer, by leaving the territory or staying around for more fun and games.

The Blue Tit has a more obvious display that, once you recognise it for what it is, becomes quite a feature of the early spring garden scene. It's not a very complicated manoeuvre, just a flight of a few metres from one perch to another, powered by wing-beats that seem faster than necessary, or flavoured by the occasional glide. But it is standardised, and even noticeable to us, so we can assume that no female could possibly miss its message and its meaning.

A budding relationship? – two Blue Tits in display.

Courtship doesn't end with a few impressive stunts by a male; it's a long process. Once paired both males and females embark upon a series of pair-bonding rituals, one after the other, often repeated again and again, intensifying along with their relationship. Many of their signals and postures are as subtle as they are meaningful, and have the overall effect of bringing both birds into a synchronised state of sexual readiness. Without the fine art of courtship, one sex or another may enter the business end of the breeding season unprepared or out of synch with their partner. This is why birds that have been paired for a long period still display to each other every spring.

Gaining Ground

The other business of early spring, that of finding a territory, is closely bound up with pairing. In many birds, in fact, you cannot obtain one (a female) without the other (a territory). A bird without its own patch of ground faces the same problem as a human adolescent full of lust but with no home of his own to go to; it's not ideal. And female birds are more ruthless than teenagers; they won't give a homeless bird a second look.

In birds that pair in flocks, the

situation can be different. A Great Tit without a partner, indeed, cannot hold on to a territory; he appears to need his mate for support, even though she rarely takes much of a role in the defence of boundaries, and does not, as a rule, sing. There is, however, a fascinating record of a female that took on the singing and protective mantle when her mate was ill for a day. Perhaps this happens regularly?

Territories come with ground rules. Virtually every garden bird species must inevitably sing to get one, and must go on singing to keep its borders intact, otherwise they will be breached. Outside a bird's own territory it acts submissively, but inside it is king of its own castle, and strangers, unless they are making a challenge, defer to it. The earlier a territory is settled and established in the spring, the larger it will end up being, and the better a bird will look to rival and mate alike. The final rule of territorial ownership is an ageist one: the older and more experienced a bird is, the larger its domain will be, a refreshingly different dynamic to our own current sociological expectations.

The odd thing is, no one actually knows what a territory is for, at least ultimately. It doesn't always delineate a feeding zone, in which only the owners forage privately; even those most violently territorial aggressors, the Robins, may turn a blind eye to foraging trespassers. So what does it do? The current theory is that it helps to space birds out so that they are not all found by a predator, densely packed and nesting in much the same sorts of places, within a short space of time. The same principle might be applied to thwart U.N. weapons inspectors searching for warheads in some rogue state; better to scatter the evidence than to concentrate it incriminatingly.

Whatever they are for, they are crucial. Pity the resident species that is not established on-site by the end of this month. It will already be behind the rest, with serious implications for its prospects.

Again, as in January, febrile February is played to a backdrop of harsh and often deadly weather. Indeed, this second month of the year can be worse than the first; the days might be slightly longer, but resources are ever more depleted, with nuts and fruits diminishing and no major hatching of insect food yet. It's a month when a garden can expect more visitors than

Fallen apples are a valuable winter food source for thrushes, like this Fieldfare.

usual, not just the same faces, but strangers travelling from further afield. Winter visiting Fieldfares and Redwings, who live a nomadic lifestyle here travelling the country in search of food, often give up on wild fruits and grassland invertebrates and come into gardens instead, where they might depend on thrown out apples or other cultivated fruits. They often drop in for a few days, then go on their way again, ever restless.

The worst days and nights continue to weed out all but the best survivors among our resident birds. They have come so far, with spring just around the corner, but this final strait is a long and demanding one. Their death provides an opportunity for rivals, and vacant territories are quickly claimed, as are bereaved partners. There is absolutely no sentiment towards a lost mate or potential mate, only the need to make good the loss before breeding begins.

Indeed, birds are not sentimental creatures. If there is a word to describe the social climate of the next few months, it is fluid. Territorial boundaries will be in a constant state of change, and, perhaps surprisingly, so will relationships. Despite the apparent deference to the pair bond, despite the enormous efforts that birds put into their compatibility, despite the often desperate search for a partner and, one might assume, relief when one is found, most birds remain open to offers throughout the whole breeding season. Some birds divorce and many indulge in sexual relations outside their formalised partnerships. The maxim of the season, from beginning to end, is to maximise your productivity, irrespective of that of your soul mate.

Red Bags to a Siskin

LOOK OUT INTO the garden and watch the hanging feeder carefully. It's February, and as such, your garden is due a visit by a Siskin. Or maybe you have them already, coming in small parties, Greenfinch-like dwarfs hardly larger than Blue Tits, with bold yellow bars on their wings and streaks on their breasts and flanks. Siskins are a delight.

But if you have them, did you know you were part of a revolution? The Siskin, you see, is taking over. It used to be quite a scarce bird in Britain, except in the coniferous forests of Wales, Scotland and northern England, and was simply not considered a garden bird. Now it's everywhere, being reported in about 40% of birdwatchers' feeding stations in some years. Its breeding population increased by two-thirds in Britain between 1968 and 1991, and is still on the way up. So something special is happening to this green-hued midget.

The garden revolution began in that most un-revolutionary of outposts, Guildford in Surrey. It was 1963, and Britain was in the grip of the hardest winter for many years. For that reason or for another we don't know about, Siskins suddenly began feeding on the hanging feeders of a garden within that town, where before they had not – they weren't in gardens anywhere else. A plaque should be installed there, recording that moment of history.

Siskins are seed-eaters like all finches. They rely on two trees in particular to provide them with seeds as they open: spruce and alder. They are also one of the few appreciators in the world of cypress, including the dreaded Leylandii, hated of suburbia. What, one might ask, drew them to gardens in the 1960s, where Leylandii was mainly a future horror and where the most sophisticated bird gardeners provided peanuts and scraps?

Whatever the attraction, the habit grew. Throughout the 1960s more and more Siskins were seen in gardens, and by the end of the decade they were being recorded over much of southern England. Their spread continued in the 1970s, and by the 1980s it was no longer news to be visited by one of these colourful little birds. Now, in the early part of the twenty-first century, one in ten gardens belonging to birdwatchers is likely to report a visit in the course of a winter. They come in groups of a few to fifty or more, stay for days, and take the

The Siskin is an agile, lively little finch, quite different in character to the heftier, more phlegmatic Greenfinch.

smaller and softer seeds that we provide. To be honest, if you don't have Siskins, you probably should not confess it to members of your bird club.

Let us return to the 1960s, however, and take a look at one of the more entertaining theories for the Siskin's success. If you were a dedicated feeder of birds then, you'll remember that peanuts used to come in red mesh bags, not in plastic feeders. That was the way it was back then, when it wasn't just the people swinging, but the birds, too – in the breeze. One day a bright spark had a stunning realisation: alder seeds, the Siskin's winter staple, are found in little hanging baskets too, small catkins of a reddish hue. Could it be the birds made the connection between their favourite little red hanging feeders and the huge, peanut-filled ones? It's plausible, with a bit of a leap of faith. You can imagine the Siskin's reaction at seeing such a red feeder, twenty times the size of a normal one. Could it have believed its eyes?

It's a nice theory but, like many of the best, impossible to prove and perhaps a little too colourful. But whatever the reason, one thing is certain; the Siskin has never looked back.

The Dance of the Dunnock

IT WASN'T LONG ago that the Dunnock or "Hedge Sparrow" was considered to be a rather uninteresting small brown bird. But since the 1980s, when it was first studied in detail, its exploits have become a red-hot topic of conversation across garden fences, and attracted more smutty headlines than those of a bed-hopping soap star. The Dunnock, you see, hides a distinctly lively lifestyle behind its veneer of ordinariness and homeliness. It's all to do with sex, of course. What else could it possibly be?

Things start to subvert right from the earliest days of spring. The females, not the males as expected, start to mark out borders and skirmish over territories in an unusual demonstration of Girl Power. The winners sit defiantly in their territories and invite the males outside to move in with them. Not surprisingly, the invitees oblige with delirious enthusiasm, and fight amongst themselves for this unexpected privilege.

Now sometimes – just sometimes – the latter dispute is a simple one, and a single male Dunnock wins the battle to move in with a single female Dunnock. If so, they share the territory completely and the male takes over its defence. They become a monogamous pair and go about the breeding season without interruption from outside. About a third of Dunnock unions turn out this way.

But more frequently, there is a two-pronged problem. In the average Dunnock population there are fewer females than males and, logically enough, with a reduced density of population, the females have relatively large territories. Unfortunately the males, with a much higher population density, have more pressure on their borders and cannot normally defend as much area as the females. So, although a certain male

A male Dunnock "wing-waving" – his threat display towards another male.

Dunnocks lend truth to the saying about the quiet ones being the worst – these soberly plumaged and softly-spoken birds have a convoluted private life worthy of any soap opera.

might take over the defence of part of a female's patch, he normally finds himself unable to defend all of it. To solve the problem he reluctantly allows another male in to keep the baying hordes outside.

It's hardly an ideal arrangement. Two males are, metaphorically speaking, flat-sharing with the same female. They defend the territory as a team, using the same song-posts and keeping within the same boundaries, but they both view the female through the same primeval steamed-up lens of intense desire. They become bitter love rivals.

Alpha Males and Beta Males

Their arrangement leads to an intense power struggle, resolving eventually into a dominance relationship between the two of them, a kind of personal peck-order, with the slightly stronger and fitter bird coming out on top. (On the rare occasions that male birds match each other with almost total equality, they often fight to the death instead.) The dominant bird, the alpha male, holds a certain sway over his subordinate, the beta male, in regard to access to the female. Having won his rights, he tries to monopolise the female's company and keep her as his exclusive sexual partner.

But it rarely works out as the alpha male

intends, not least because of the unexpected motivations of his female! The female seems reluctant to be monopolised, and actually goes out of her way to encourage the beta male to go behind his master's back and, shall we say, meet her behind the bike sheds. She actively seeks sexual relations with both birds, even as both males are firmly in competition against each other. The garden lawn is the floor, then, for a curious dance of the Dunnocks, in which a female dashes back and forth between her suitors, one relationship open and freely acknowledged, the other enigmatic and merely suspected.

Why should she do this? The motivations of the males are clear enough, each bird wishing to promote its paternity by keeping the female's attentions to itself. But why should the female be so solicitous to both admirers? The reason is surprisingly straightforward: in return for copulation, each male effectively signs a contract stating that he will help with feeding the young. In a situation where food might be difficult to find, the help of an extra shopper could be a significant boost to a female's chicks' chances of survival.

. . . And Gammas too

So here is a pertinent but explosive question: if two, why not three? Could they? Yes they could. Some Dunnock territories contain three males, alpha, beta and gamma, all competing for a single female's affections. Such chicks are mightily well fed, and the female could almost go part-time, but for the males it means that they are condemned to a stressful, and perhaps disappointing breeding season.

Sometimes, though, the Dance of the Dunnocks follows a different step. From time to time, "alpha-plus" males arise in a population, birds that can indeed monopolise a female's territory - and not just one, but two. Perhaps these super-males result in years when the female population density is greater than usual and these hold consequently smaller territories; or perhaps some males are just born to be superior. Whatever their origin, these birds find the defence of a single female's territory so easy that they have a go at defending two, and if they succeed they monopolise both females. That's a great arrangement for them, but it naturally reduces the help that each female can expect in the task of looking after the young. Although that would appear to give the females a more difficult time, at least they have the compensation of knowing that their young will come from strong, vigorous stock. Forget the help; feel the genes.

But not all potential "alpha-plus" males are quite as superior as they might seem at first. At the beginning they can exclude all other males from two female territories, but over the weeks their stranglehold begins to loosen, and they are eventually forced to share the defence of the two territories with a second or even third male. The arrangement is the same as in the flat-share described above, with each of the males involved in a dominance relationship: an alpha, beta and gamma male. The only difference is that there are now two females involved, and things begin to get complicated. Both females attempt to mate with each male, but at the same time the alpha male will try to prevent it happening, and monopolise both females for himself. But he is now acting against the wishes of not only the beta male and the possible gamma male, but also both females! So he rarely succeeds. Four or five in a flat allows for plenty of playing around.

Finally, in rare cases two males might find that joining forces to defend the territories of two females is so easy that they might as well try defending three, or even four adjacent female territories. If this happens, each female can be fairly guaranteed two helpers, and the males can

bicker between themselves as to who mates with whom.

What is so remarkable about Dunnocks is not that they frequently have multiple partners – lots of birds do that. It is because all their sexual liaisons are formalised, with both sexes having a role, rather than being quick flings outside an essentially monogamous relationship. These are not extra-pair copulations; they are copulations with extra mates.

When all this was discovered, the scientists struggled with terminology. A combination of one male and one female had long been known as monogamy, and the combination of one sex with two or more members of the opposite sex as polygamy: polygyny when it was one male with multiple mates, and polyandry when it was one female with multiple mates. The Dunnock, though, has forced a new word to find its way into the dictionary: polygynandry, the system in which, for example, a male can be polygynous with females that are themselves polyandrous. There are not many garden birds, small brown or otherwise, whose escapades have been so singular as to require the invention of a new word and a new concept.

What is more, the Dance of the Dunnocks is going on in your back garden, perhaps even right now. And there isn't a thing you can do about it.

If a female Dunnock has two males to help her at the nest, her chicks have a greatly improved chance of survival.

The Crow's Nest

IT ONLY TAKES a few days of mild February weather to start the crows nesting. They break sticks off branches and carry them to the top of a tree in their bills, laying them down and intertwining them into a platform. It's only a beginning, but this pile of sticks puts down a marker of residence for the breeding season. It's now the crows' lair and the shadow of these fierce creatures will fall long and dark over the gardens below for the next few months. A crow's nest is like one of those frightening castles to which comic-book heroines are inevitably taken when captured: high, fortress-like places from which the baddies rule and where only the bravest go.

But crow's nests are also architectural marvels. That high rise structure we see in the tall trees around our houses is not some draughty pallet-like platform; it will soon have far more in common with the sumptuousness of a penthouse suite, albeit a cup-shaped one. It will actually consist of four layers of different materials, all brought in with great care in their turn and lovingly moulded into shape to make a strong but elastic structure, well able to withstand strong winds. The crow's nest, combining twigs, roots, stalks, grass and feathers, is strong, resilient and warm inside.

We don't normally associate crows with such wholesome qualities as craftsmanship, care and skill. Instead we tend to loathe them, with their unyielding black plumage, fierce looks and tendency to harm the weak and sick of other species. Our dislike of them has a long history. Way back in time before gardens became places of leisure, they would attend the gallows and the overflowing graveyards of the Great Plague, picking off what was left of lifeless human bodies. They might have acquired good meals at the time, but it was a Medieval P.R. disaster.

And yet, the Carrion Crow could be loved and admired, if its less wholesome habits were somehow overlooked. As well as being a great craftsman, it is also blessed with high intelligence. In the wild it has learned to drop shells on to a hard surface to crack them open, for example. And, remarkably, crows "play". Adults have often been seen riding the skies and mock-fighting for the sheer "fun" of it, and juveniles

A pair of crows in their treetop fortress.

have been watched sliding down sloping roofs again and again like daring toddlers.

Somehow, though, a bird's intelligence is not always a quality important to garden watchers. Perhaps cleverness is too dismissive of frailty, the quality that, deep down, we know we all have. Whatever it is, the crow's apparent ease with life is perhaps the most powerful argument against indulgent appreciation and regard.

Stress and Tensions

But here we are mistaken. The Carrion Crow, despite a veneer of mastery, is in fact a bird that leads a life brim-full of difficulties and stresses, with few spells of ease. Magpies, for example, hate Carrion Crows with a rabid passion, and the two species undertake a mutual campaign of harassment wherever they live close to each other. Tensions run high all season.

Another unsavoury mutual enmity seethes between territorial Carrion Crows and the floating population that drifts around in non-breeding flocks. In an average population, you see, there are not enough territories to keep everybody happy. Some birds are landed, whilst the rest gather in resentful gangs. If a pair of Carrion Crows builds their nest in a place that the non-breeding flock don't like, the ne'er-do-wells will sometimes make raids upon it and cause its destruction.

And no territorial crow can ever feel entirely established. If it feels below par, it is immediately under pressure. And if it loses a partner, it is on borrowed time. Crows have no pity. Any sick bird is simply disinherited, sometimes with shocking expeditiousness. And if a territorial male dies, it can enter the ranks of the forgotten within a couple of hours. Such are the pressures of crow society that new owners can move in on the same afternoon.

So, whatever we think of crows, we should not assume that they have everything their own way. They dish out violence, and they receive it back with a vengeance. As garden watchers we will certainly never love them, but perhaps at least we can sympathise with them a little, siding as we love to with the downtrodden and the underdog.

For up there, in its apparently impregnable treetop fortress, the Carrion Crow lives life on an uncertain edge.

Bullfinches as Pests

IT'S THE SEASON of buds, and mild-mannered gardeners everywhere are getting hot under the collar about Bullfinches. For the rest of the year these heavily built, boldly coloured finches are welcomed into the garden and enjoyed for the intensity of their colours. But in the early spring both sexes, the male with a cherry-red breast and the female, more soberly coloured in plum, are the scourge of the fruit grower and the lover of blossom. With their favourite tree-seeds now exhausted in the wider countryside, these mild-mannered beauties turn their attention to soft vegetable matter. And the best place to find that is in gardens and orchards.

If you find yourself running outside and shaking your fist helplessly at one of these bud-guzzlers, you can be assured that it was ever thus. Bullfinches have been irritating people for about five hundred years. In the sixteenth century every Bullfinch had a price on its head: a penny was awarded for 'everie Bulfynche…that devoureth the blowthe of fruit'. And do they devour: a Bullfinch can eat up to forty-five buds a minute, and will strip a whole branch during a single surreptitious visit to your well tended fruit trees.

Choosy Visitors

Buds and blossoms don't yield much energy. It might be no consolation to the owner of an affected fruit-tree, but the Bullfinches would far rather be feeding on something else. They would prefer to be consuming ash seeds, for example, a special favourite of theirs. But the ash tree is a fickle plant: some years yield an excellent crop, enough to keep Bullfinches out of mischief far into the spring, but other years are more disappointing, forcing the birds to look elsewhere. So bullfinches are as reluctant guests in your garden as you are host.

At one time the Bullfinch's potential threat to the livelihoods of commercial fruit growers was recognised by law, and in the hotspots of south-east England and the Midlands it was possible to cull Bullfinches on licence. The problem was that, when the Bullfinch consumed the flower buds, it destroyed the chance of the same bit of branch fruiting later in the season. The culling never did much good, though, because the bountiful crop

drew birds from a wide area, and the same numbers kept on coming year after year. Studies showed that the birds were particularly choosy, preferentially going for certain types of buds, and indeed even for certain varieties. The main damage caused was to pears, plums (especially Golden Gage) and gooseberries between January and March, and to blackcurrants a little later. Much less harm came to crops of apples.

Since a peak in the 1950s to the 1970s, however, the Bullfinch population in Britain has fallen into decline, and fruit growers now hardly ever see significant damage by these broad-billed birds. The species has now been taken off the general licence to control, making culling illegal, and where once the Bullfinch was regarded as an agricultural pest, it is now a cause for conservation concern. The cause has nothing to do with buds or orchards, though. It is almost certainly the result of the wide-scale destruction of hedgerows, and the modern intensification of farming, with the resultant loss of seed-yielding weeds such as nettles, docks and dandelions, which Bullfinches love.

With the species in retreat, it is now difficult to justify resenting its periodic intrusions into our gardens. Not only is the Bullfinch beautiful, but it is becoming scarce, too. If you fruit-tree cultivators should require further consolation, then be aware that most Bullfinches do no major damage at all, even when they do occupy the gardens for a few weeks in the early spring. It takes a 50% reduction of a tree's buds to have any impact on its fruit yield in that season, and that's a lot of work required by a lot of Bullfinches. There will be plenty left over.

In the last few years Bullfinches, ironically, have begun to come into gardens in much larger numbers, not because of buds but because of bird tables. They were once so shy, and had so many other options available, that they avoided too

much contact with
people. But now, it appears,
they have little choice. With wild
food dwindling in the wild they have been
learning to visit feeding stations, as so many other
birds have, and have been forced to be less reticent.
Now you are as likely to see them tucking into
black sunflower seeds as you are buds.

So now you have a solution to the Bullfinches'
eating buds in your garden. Give them a good
meal elsewhere, and the damage will be
insignificant. It's a pity they didn't realise that
five hundred years ago.

*Most finch species visit food sources in flocks, but not the
Bullfinch. It goes around in pairs or small groups,
turning up among the buds and blossoms without fanfare.*

BY MARCH the spring is truly old news. The Go-Ahead Bird is already satisfactorily paired, and settled into a territory. It knows its neighbours by song, and its place in the world. A bird entering March without a border and a partner is like a student taking final exams without having done any revision: a pass is a possibility, but it is leaving success perilously to chance.

MARCH

The Early Bird

MARCH MIGHT QUALIFY as the early part of the spring, but for most birds the preliminaries of breeding are already over. The real question to be faced now is not so much how to enter the next stage of the reproductive cycle, but when to do it. Many pairs will in theory be in a state of readiness, but may wait until the following month before finally building a nest and laying eggs. The onset of nesting is a very individual affair, with much depending on how each pair has fared through the winter season, and the effects of the weather.

March, though, at last relieves the stark shortage of natural food in the garden. On the trees, the leaf buds are being munched by newly hatched caterpillars, the first of the year. A few somnolent bees fly about the daffodils and daisies, small insects emerge from the pussy willows, and midges begin to dance in the shelter-belts. A host of small creatures come out of the litter, metaphorically yawning and blinking in the rays of the newly confident sun.

Warmer days this month seethe with activity from dawn to dusk. The mornings are taken up with busy foraging - Blackbirds finding worms on the lawn, Pied Wagtails fielding insects from sunlit roofs, and Chaffinches searching the boughs of trees. The days are punctuated by displays of various kinds, from the intimate and perch-bound to the aerial and effervescent. And as evening falls, there is another bout of earnest foraging, everybody filling up in the last of the light. Nobody wants to be caught out by a cold night, not now with milder conditions at last in sight.

But the general appearance of contentment and vigour masks a stark inequality among bird populations. Some individuals have emerged from the winter much fitter than others. They are the ones to forge ahead into nest-building, while others must wait and feed up. Some are ready to go, others are not.

In bird society, it is inevitably the older, more experienced birds that hold this advantage and make up the majority of the early nesters. They and their partners may get underway two or three weeks before the juniors of their species, and have eggs in the nest before their rivals have even started to build. As we've seen, these oldies hold larger territories than the youngsters and they obtain a mate, on average, much more quickly. They display with greater ardour and vigour when approached by a prospective partner, and have better, more enticing songs. Everything points towards their superiority. Old is best.

None of this should be surprising. A bird in its first winter of life is a complete novice; it has never faced the cold season before. It has

Previous page: Mistle Thrushes nest building.

Left: The Chiffchaff is one of the first migrant birds to arrive in spring.

needed to discover how to forage effectively, what to eat and what to avoid, how to search in the right places, how to find a suitable roosting site. By contrast, the older birds already know the ropes. They have been through these difficulties before, and have cut all the corners the rookies couldn't find. Their bellies have been fuller more often and they are in good condition. The young birds are certainly the winners of their generation, having survived at all, but they aren't ready for all the new challenges just yet.

To these older birds, then, starting early is a goal and a priority. The great advantage to them, of course, is that by setting the pace they might squeeze more breeding attempts into a season than would otherwise be possible, and produce more young overall – that, of course, is the object of the whole exercise of breeding, maximising your productivity. The senior birds might, for example, produce three broods of four young, instead of two. That's quite an inducement.

Jumping the Gun

However, running your advance laps at full pace carries great risks along with these enticements. The early bird may catch a cold as well as a worm. Breeding takes up an enormous amount of effort – think how many trips a bird must take to bring food to its young – and depends for its success on a good food supply, which is not guaranteed in March or April. This can put a bird in danger. If, for example, a male is trying to juggle feeding itself with singing to protect its territory, it might compromise its needs too much, and die on a cold March night. Even the fittest overstretch themselves.

They are, in a sense, fighting against a gradient. If birds are to breed early, they need to get into peak condition by eating heartily. But the garden's productivity is not at its peak; food will be much more abundant later on. At the very time they need more food than usual, they have to search for it that much harder. That's their conundrum, and their risk. Yet it's also their proving ground, and their opportunity. Speculators may have spectacular failures, but it is they, not those that hesitate, who get rich quick.

There is another consideration in breeding early, though, and that is to the hatching generation. There is no point starting to breed if, when your young eventually leave the nest, there won't be enough food around for them to survive. That

A male Starling delivers his mish-mash of a song on an early spring morning.

would be a waste of effort; it would be better to hang on and wait. When the odds are stacked too heavily against them, birds simply don't breed: natural selection eliminates those that try.

Within every population of birds there are early starters and late risers, but of course different species also follow different regimes. Tits, for example, always withhold laying their eggs before April, because any earlier would be too soon to coincide with the predictable bloom of caterpillar food on which their young depend. Sparrowhawks are late starters too because they will be feeding their young on the new generation of those self-same tits. Tit fledglings are essentially fast food, easy to catch and satisfactorily nutritious, ideal for growing predators-to-be. It's worth the wait.

But quite a few birds do typically get well underway during March: birds as different as Tawny Owls, Mistle Thrushes and Rooks are likely to be sitting on eggs by the middle of the month. They each have their own reasons for beginning early, and each reason is a demonstration of how finely interwoven the natural community is, even in a garden.

Take the Tawny Owl, for example. It's a predator on many creatures, including birds, but it prefers to bring small mammals, such as voles, mice and rats, to its hungry young. Although there are always plenty of these around, especially during the summer, they are not always easy to catch once the ground where they live is covered with a copious growth of grass, herbs and other vegetation. So the Tawny Owls time their breeding so that they can catch the bulk of their youngsters' food when the grass is low and rodents are vulnerable.

The case of the Mistle Thrush is less clear cut, and the theories surrounding it a little speculative. The idea is that Mistle Thrushes start early to avoid predation. They make large, quite

conspicuous nests, placed higher up than those of most birds, and hence potentially vulnerable. But in March, so the argument goes, not many crows or Sparrowhawks have yet 'got into' nest-robbing; they are finding food elsewhere. So the Mistle Thrushes make what progress they can before the predators start seriously snooping around.

Rookies and Rooks

No one can miss a rookery, and in more rural gardens the activities of Rooks around their colonies are an unmistakable sign of spring. For Rooks an early start is necessary so that they can avoid bringing up their nestlings in the summer months of June and July. By then the ground will be drying out and the young Rooks' staple food, earthworms, will burrow deeper into the soil, becoming much harder to reach. It would be virtually impossible to raise young under such conditions, but in the early spring, when breeding starts, suitable food abounds.

A rookery in March is alive with sound and excitement. Birds come and go from their treetop nests, causing caws of welcome from their mate when they arrive and at the same time caws of reproach from their neighbours, as if they had parked their cars blocking an oft-used drive. Every few minutes birds bring sticks into their nests, threading them in, then trying somewhere else, seemingly never quite happy with the construction, forever altering materials in a constant state of fuss and refurbishment. Males are bowing, females are sitting; everyone has a great

deal to say. The colony is busy, noisy, and soon gets dirty, making it a kind of Rook town centre with throbbing traffic and short-tempered inhabitants.

A Migrant Marathon

So March resounds to the beat of productivity. Alongside the habitual early nesters are the vanguard of Robins, Blackbirds, Song Thrushes, and sundry other species. These are, remember, the high achievers in your garden, the older and familiar faces.

Way down to the south of us, another contest is raging. It is just as intense as the competition already obvious in the garden, as birds squabble over territories and mates. And again, in common with the other battles, it is invariably won by older, more experienced individuals. This contest is between migrants, and is effectively a race, with hundreds of individual birds each aiming to be among the first of its kind to arrive on its breeding grounds.

The mix of birds in the garden is about to change. The summer visitors are well on their way, with the first reaching these shores in March. Every garden watcher feels a jolt of excitement when seeing their first Swallow of the season, and there will be many similar appointments in the coming weeks. Your most likely first arrival will be probably be a Chiffchaff, a small, rather plain, olive-green warbler, easy to miss, that will flit busily around in your herbaceous border, taking time off between courses to utter its name in song, 'Chiff-chaff-chiff-chaff…' with a preoccupied air.

The birds' migration has been a marathon. Having set off from Africa (Swallows) or southern Europe (Chiffchaffs) at about the same time as their peers, the front-runners have left their competitors far behind over the weeks of their journey. Their fitness determines their arrival date and, just as it does for the resident birds, their haste determines how large their territory will be, with the winners establishing larger patches than the pack behind them. As a rule, the earlier a migratory bird arrives, the better its chance of breeding success.

So the scene is set for a new season of replication, of nests, eggs and young. Already our well mannered gardens are rife with inequality and discord, and it's only going to get worse.

The Long-tailed Tit's Building Programme

IF YOU HAVE Long-tailed Tits in your garden, you might have noticed something unusual recently. Where are all the flocks? They have disintegrated. A few weeks ago you would never have seen fewer than six of these small birds together at a time; but now you don't. The flocks have split up, and their components have paired off. The basic Long-tailed Tit unit is now just two.

It's odd, this splitting off, because each of the various pairs is now facing a task of gigantic proportions; a task, ironically, that could have been easier to do with a bit of teamwork, with a bit of help from the kinfolk. It's the building of a large and intricate outdoor nest, a structure many times larger than the builders themselves, made of several different materials and requiring over three weeks of hard effort to complete. One could imagine them sitting back a little and contemplating the job in front of them like an author confronts an empty page; it is a daunting prospect.

At least they've done a bit of the work. They have chosen a site.

The nest will be low down in a bush, well hidden, and protected by the prickles of whatever vegetation they have selected. At the same time it will be placed carefully to catch the warming rays of the sun to the south. Some maverick Long-tailed Tits choose a completely different site, high in a tree, but these are in the minority.

A Firm Foundation

The labours of a pair begin in the benign sunshine of a March morning, when they do a round of the trees and logs in their territory to collect moss. Each beakful is brought to the nest site and dropped on to a thorny branch, until one or more pieces stays put to form a potential foundation. After a few more collecting trips the birds build up a small platform of moss, which stays rather precariously in place, held together by friction and gravity.

It does, however, need securing in place, and for this the Long-tailed Tits go out and find a natural adhesive. Nothing fits the bill better than strands of cobweb and, much to the chagrin of their hard-working eight-legged owners, webs are repeatedly raided. The strands of cobweb bind the moss to the branch, and now the first task, building the foundation, is complete.

The Long-tailed Tits now build walls upon their foundations, using the same two basic ingredients: moss held together by cobwebs. First they collect the moss and place it in position, and then they secure it, so the workers alternate moss and web-collecting expeditions.

A Long-tailed Tit's nest in its early stages – just a cup of moss secured with cobwebs.

carefully weaving them onto the side of the nest. They don't stop until the whole of the cup stage of the nest is completely covered; perhaps without decent camouflage the construction would soon become unacceptably conspicuous.

With this first lichen-covering task complete the nest is about a third finished. It is now a shallow cup, and needs to become a dome. The same building technique proceeds as before, with moss-and-web sessions being alternated with trips to collect lichen. The cup walls grow higher and higher until they are taller than the birds themselves. And now, since the birds cannot reach the rim it begins, inevitably, to lean over and takes its place as the roof. With a few specialised weaving routines the roof is bound together at

The birds sit on the platform for the web-weaving part, and as they weave the birds turn round slowly, like feathered clock hands denoting the hour until, after many days of hard work, the birds have produced a cup.

Above: A Long-tailed Tit places lichen over its nest cup to camouflage it.

Below: Almost complete – the pair brings in feathers for insulation.

Finishing Touches

The Long-tailed Tits now turn their attention to a quite different ingredient: lichen. Where moss and spider's webs are the equivalent of bricks and mortar respectively, the lichen is like pebbledash or stucco, an outside finish for the construction. Lichens offer excellent camouflage when sprinkled over the nest, and the birds concentrate on collecting them for a period of several days,

Death brings life – a Woodpigeon's demise is a Long-tailed Tit's opportunity.

the top, the entrance hole is completed and at last, after weeks of effort, the nest begins to look like a finished product.

But it's not finished. Arguably the most fascinating part of the nest building is still to come. The Long-tailed Tits shift their attention to a new ingredient for their nest and to a new style of collecting. From now on, they will concentrate entirely upon gathering feathers.

Counts vary, but a Long-tailed Tits' nest will eventually be filled with between nine hundred and two thousand feathers. Virtually all of them are stuffed inside the structure, although a few are also placed around the entrance hole to offer a little extra concealment. These feathers act as superb insulation for the chicks: even though, on a hot day, it must become almost unbearable inside with eight small bodies and the brooding female crammed amongst them.

The really intriguing question is not how many feathers a pair of Long-tailed Tits might use for the nest, but where do they get them from? Certainly not from their own bodies: in March or April they cannot spare them. From bird roosts? – certainly. From chicken coops? – very likely. But what about in gardens, or in the wildwoods where feathers don't lie around much in spring?

Where can the birds go to find this valuable resource?

In many cases the answer would appear to be a bit creepy: they go to the morgue, or at least to a recently killed bird. Long-tailed Tits don't have the physical ability to form hit-squads and knock off ideally-plumaged birds such as pigeons when they need to. But instead they must monitor the garden dramas around them with unusual alertness, and detect when a predator has made a kill and take their chance when it comes. Perhaps the most extraordinary thing about the Long-tailed Tits' intricate construction is that it often requires the death of another bird to enable it to be finished off. From a death springs an opportunity.

The Long-tailed Tit's building programme is a three-week long project that sees at its end the construction of a minor marvel. Using four very different materials, several of them quite scarce, the birds somehow manage to produce a structure that is perfectly adapted for its job: strong, flexible, warm and perfectly fitted.

Many of us who have experienced renovations in our gardens might allow ourselves a wry smile when we look at these tiny birds' efficiency. If only all builders were as good as this!

Wrens as Property Developers

WRENS ARE SMALL birds with big mouths. Their songs are incredibly loud, their bodies incredibly tiny. It's a relief that other birds – and people! – don't make sounds in similar proportion to their size; otherwise we'd all be deaf.

But Wrens need to make a noise. They live among the thickest tangles of vegetation, a hidden, twilight world where only the small-bodied can go. To them grass is a forest, herbaceous borders are the size of counties, and the garden goes as far as the horizon will stretch. In their world it is dark and impenetrable and safe. The only way they can contact each other is by singing loudly.

Throughout the year every male does just that, defending his territory with vocal vigour. As the spring approaches the pressure on property increases, and the gardens and woods become places where noise pollution is at its worst just a short distance above the ground, where the Wrens battle it out. It's intense and it's vociferous, but

the result of all this early spring shouting is to leave each male with a patch of ground that he can call his own.

Like human young adults, male Wrens soon accept female visitors to their property. The females come and go and cause much excitement. Host and guest chase, curtsey and quiver their wings to express a mutual interest. Hormones circulate.

About this time the male Wren encounters a raging urge. 'Build a nest!' his body chemistry squeals. And he does. Then he builds another. It feels good, so he builds still another. And another. Some time later exhaustion, either of body or motivation, eventually brings his building spree to an end, but by then he has constructed as many as ten nests within his territory, more than fulfilling his initial urge.

Now these are very much male nests. They are, indeed, often called 'cock nests', since they are exclusively built by the cock bird. But they are only

A male Wren belts out his song towards a visiting female, his body trembling like an opera singer.

really the shells of nests, the outer walls of a Wren-style dome built up of moss, grass and dead leaves. They could really do with a little subtlety, especially for the inner décor. If our Wren were a person we would say that his work needed a feminine touch.

Funnily enough, the Wren agrees. With his handiwork complete, he now has something to show off to his visitors. They come as they did before, but this time, in addition to the courtship preliminaries, they will be given a nest to inspect.

The Female's Choice

Now you know what it's like when you are showing off a piece of work that you've created, especially to a potential mate. It's possible to become very excited, very animated and a little over the top. The male Wren is a victim of this, too. He lures the visiting female with courtship songs, moving a few hops ahead of her in the direction of the nest as, little by little, it is about to be revealed. He sings loudly, hops around with itchy feet, spreads and quivers his wings, and generally becomes intoxicated. When the nest finally comes into view, he seems almost to lose his head. He dashes headlong into the dome and there he waits, sometimes for several minutes, before hopping out again, giving excited calls. 'Come in,' he might be saying, 'it's spacious enough for a growing family'.

The female is highly reticent about the nest at first. Perhaps she senses the importance of the moment. She simply peers in from a distance. But, then, having come this far, she has a look in, and the male buzzes around her, almost incandescent with excitement.

No one knows what exactly goes on inside a female Wren's head at this time, but this is the moment that she says 'yea' or 'nay' in her heart. Either her breeding season begins here, or she must look elsewhere. And in case you're wondering – yes, it is as much the nest she's choosing as the potential mate that built it. Its structure tells her all she needs to know.

If her answer is 'yes', the female stays around, and soon both sexes spend some time inside their dome. If it's a 'no', the female's first cursory inspection will be her last. The successful male Wren very soon becomes acquainted with his female, in every sense of the word. They copulate

The male wren starts the building, but it is the female who collects food for the chicks.

very close to the nest that forged their bond.

As it turns out the female is wise to be choosy about home rather than home-maker. She won't see much more of him from now on, unless he's the overseeing type. Some males are; some aren't. Either way, she won't be expecting him to share much of the hard work to come. She will complete the nest by lining it, with feathers or fine hairs. She will lay the eggs, incubate them and brood the young by herself. When the eggs hatch she will feed the chicks almost entirely on her own, with little or no contribution from her mate. Only when they have left the nest and begun roaming uncertainly about the neighbourhood will he then keep watch over the fledglings and offer them portions of food. But, quite honestly, the female expected this. It's her young she was thinking about. If her chosen mate has a good nest in a good territory, her young are assured that essential well fed start to life.

The male is not lazy; he has a reason to be inattentive. You see, while his mate is busy with her tasks, from his perspective the breeding season is as yet young, and for him it still holds rich possibilities. Like every cock bird, a male Wren's dream each season is to maximise the number of young that he can possibly sire. That could mean attracting another mate or two to his territory.

He didn't build just the one nest, remember. He has plenty of properties on the market yet to be inspected. And there are female Wrens out there that could well be interested in a paired male with a good territory.

Male Wrens, you see, are like property developers. They 'buy' their land and build on it. They don't need to make money like the human kind, but gain instead by attracting females and ensuring their genes are passed on to as many young as possible. Wrens nest for success.

Keep Feeding!

IN YEARS GONE by we all stopped feeding birds in the early spring. 'The insects are coming out now,' was the perceived wisdom, 'and the birds can look after themselves.'

If we went on beyond April we were accused of murder. 'Whatever you do,' said the sages, 'don't let the tits get to the peanuts. They will feed them to their young and the young will choke when the nuts get stuck in their throats.' Guiltily, the bird table was taken down, and the bird food thrown away.

How things have changed! Now there are glossy brochures for bird food companies, and we can get our stocks from the supermarket instead of the pet shop. We are urged to keep feeding (and to keep spending). 'The birds,' say our modern day gurus, 'need your help, at all times of the year. Don't let them down!'

Well, one thing's for sure and that's that the birds haven't changed. They successfully lived from March to July without our help before we deigned to give it, and they can still do so today. The rest is our choice, to withhold it or to give it. The bird populations are probably less affected than our pleasure and our purses.

Spring Shortage

That said, the days of early spring are a very difficult time for birds in the garden. Stocks of food in the wider countryside have had all winter to decline, and are running low. True, the insects are coming out again, but that is scant consolation to a seed-eater, or a bird that needs a lot of food now. The apparently relieving months of March and April are among the very worst for supplying naturally what birds need.

So that's a good reason to keep buying from those catalogues. And here's another. To get into breeding condition a bird needs to eat far more than it otherwise would. By providing food artificially in our gardens we make good any natural shortfall that might hold our birds back.

Well then, who can resist it? Get those seed-hoppers flowing! But hang on - what about all those baby birds, all on the cusp of being choked to death by peanuts? What do we do about them?

First of all, let's cut to the facts. There has never been convincing evidence that baby birds choked on peanuts – at least not on an epidemic scale.

The Nuthatch – one of many species that can benefit from artificial feeding in spring and summer.

The birds at the centre of the scare were tits. Young tits eat caterpillars, which their parents are programmed to provide. Perhaps these unfortunate incidents occurred when caterpillars were scarce and peanuts were all that was available. But choking remains at least a possibility, and we should hate to see it happen. So, just to be on the safe side, the diligent bird gardener should supply peanuts in a fine wire mesh, obliging the adults to peck out small pieces rather than removing whole nuts. Alternatively the peanuts can be ground up into small pieces before being fed to the birds. That will keep everyone happy.

There's a further consideration. When parent birds are feeding young they are under considerable physical stress themselves. It's hard enough trying to feed ten mouths when you're hungry yourself. By providing food artificially in the breeding season, we can help the birds feed the birds - the adults can gorge themselves on our food and then fly off to find whatever their chicks need. So everyone benefits.

It looks, then, as though the wisdom of old was wrong. Feeding in the summer is the new rock 'n' roll. The birds benefit, the bird gardener benefits.

And the bird food companies benefit, too. Now, where was that bribe they promised me...?

Chansons d'Amour?

BY THE END of March we don't need to know that it's spring. The birds tell us, with loud voices. Every dawn is met by a chorus that envelops the cold, damp atmosphere and shakes it awake, while each day broadcasts non-stop high-pitched tunes as incessantly as a department store at Christmas.

And we humans love it. Spring bird song is a wonder, and it gladdens our hearts. The birds sound so joyful and high spirited it is tempting to think that they are expressing their sheer delight at being alive, especially as we hear them against the colourful backdrop of those freshly rinsed greens, blues and yellows of the new season.

But actually they aren't. Our singing and bird songs are not the same. Bird song is not the light-spirited affair we think it is, or sounds like.

Songs as Magnets

In the fiercely competitive world of the garden bird, song is really just another tool for forging ahead in the breeding race. It is almost exclusive to males, and has a uniquely dual purpose: on the one hand, it declares ownership of a territory to other males, keeping them away; and on the other, it attracts females. Often the same song does both. So bird song could be thought of as a magnet, attracting material of a different polarity, but repelling its own.

The bird chorus, then, so high-pitched and musical, is in reality a male voice choir, consisting of highly charged territory owners telling their neighbours and rivals to buzz off. Songs are heavy with threat and full of grim intent.

But at least they act as a first warning. By singing a bird puts down a marker, like a musical version of a flag placed in the ground by a prospector. A marker can be challenged, but over time, if the singer is persistent, it will become set in the corporate consciousness. By listening to one another, and assessing each other's songs, birds can establish an order of things without having to resort to too much physical confrontation over territory. Visual displays and fights do occur, but song is the first buffer against this, and has a civilising influence. Singing spaces males into territories without too much bloodshed.

And at the same time, songs are of beguiling

fascination to females. Singing is a shameless universal declaration of availability, like a bachelor's site on the open air internet. A female can listen to males trading vocal punches, and draw an impression of each one's capabilities, and their potential as a mate.

It must make for exceptionally fervent listening, for the singing males are laying themselves bare. They perform to the limit of their abilities, and their audience is well aware of this. By singing, each soloist discloses honest information, conveying his age, experience, vigour and perhaps marital status. A human female would crave for such ready information in the public domain!

This disclosure of vital statistics underlines the fact that every song is different. Although birds of a certain species may all sound identical to us, they aren't. If we listen with particular care, we

A singing Blackbird is not enjoying itself, no matter what we may think. Singing is stressful and hard.

can begin to pick out the different individuals by their distinct phrases and by the frequency of favourite 'words' or syllables. For just as people have their own distinctive voices, so do Blackbirds, Great Tits and Chaffinches, and we can learn to recognise them as we do each other. Different males have their own repertoires, some richer and more varied than others. So spring song is a very public demonstration of a particular male's strengths and weaknesses.

And that, in essence, is what a song is for. We might expect a bird's singing to convey joy and love, but in fact it does something much more important. It identifies its singer to the core of its being, allowing every listener to make a judgement of it, from its peers and rivals to its human audience revelling in the melody of it all.

APRIL IS a month with a loud soundtrack. No male bird with pretensions towards reproduction can keep its mouth shut at this time of year. The atmosphere is always heavy with song, ready to drench any listener who steps outside.

APRIL

Solos and Duets

BY APRIL, ANY male with a decent song should have firmly secured his territorial borders. His neighbours know his tune well and keep a respectful distance, leaving the singer and his mate to live in relative peace within their hard won patch of ground. But it's an uneasy truce, and any break now in the male's vocal output would be disastrous. It would be the equivalent of cutting short an advertising campaign in the human world - suddenly your name would slip from the public's mind, and your competitors would win out. In the same way an avian singing slouch would soon lose territory, mate and opportunity. He cannot afford to fall silent.

That's why now, and right up until June or July, many species keep on singing their solos. It takes considerable effort, and in some birds such as Song Thrushes, Nuthatches and Chaffinches, it probably precludes males from taking part in such activities as nest-building and incubating young. The singing male and the hard-pressed female would appear to divide their tasks unequally, yet the territorial song is the licence for everything.

A Place to Nest

Somewhere safe within their vocally defined borders, many a pair of birds will begin at about this time of year to construct a tangible structure: the nest. All over the garden, from mud in the flowerbeds to grass clippings on the compost-heap, from old leaves under shrubs to moss growing on the side of a stone, building materials are being moved by dozens of busy bills.

It is tempting to view nests as 'homes', where birds live, come back from work and put their feet up. But in reality, a nest is a dangerous place, a potential trap. Once linked to one, birds that are normally highly mobile, evasive and unpredictable become much more calculable and vulnerable to predators. But of course, a nest is essential. If it does nothing else, it keeps all the eggs together, so the parent birds know where they are, and where they should focus their attentions. When a bird is incubating, the nest

also helps to keep the eggs under the 'brood patch', an area of a bird's belly from which feathers are shed so that the shells make direct contact with the parent bird's skin. So in a way, nest and bird work in some sort of harmony.

A nest can be dominating and obvious, like a parish church, a centre of the community that all can see. Or, more frequently it will be hidden from view and accessible only through some secret pathway. Carrion Crows are makers of the parish church type, placing a robust stick structure commandingly high in a tree. But very few small birds build high above ground, despite a widespread perception that they use the trees. In spring and summer, the thickest greenery is found between the garden floor and a person's head height and, in consequence, so are most of the nests – Blackbirds in hedges, Greenfinches in shrubs, Wrens in ivy, Robins in banks on the ground. Although such situations are primarily selected for protection from predators, they have a secondary purpose, too – that of shelter from the elements. Greenery conceals, but also buffers wind and rain. Nests under cover are dry and snug. Nests high up get blown about, and run the risk of disintegrating or falling down.

Previous page: A male Blackbird in full song.

Right: A male Ring-necked Parakeet at its nest-hole. Holes like this are always in short supply.

A Great Tit sings outside his nest-hole at dawn, to ensure that the female is aware of his presence.

Self-contained Apartments

Of all the possible places a bird might nest, none are more popular than holes. Holes offer everything a bird needs, all in one: concealment, shelter, confinement for eggs and chicks. They are self-contained apartments, ready made for the bird market.

And the market is always on the up. Demand easily exceeds supply. The only problem, it seems, with nesting in a hole is laying claim to one in the first place. A range of species competes for them, fighting off others if necessary, including Tawny Owls, Ring-necked Parakeets, Jackdaws, Kestrels, Starlings, Tree Sparrows, Nuthatches and Blue, Great and Coal Tits, quite apart from the woodpeckers that often excavate them in the first place. Naturally, different holes suit different species – a Tawny Owl, for example, could not squeeze into a Blue Tit's ideal home. But few holes go begging for tenants in the crowded world of the garden.

The business of selecting a site is a distinctly mysterious activity, played to rules only the birds themselves know. We may find birds' choices unfathomable. We can put up apparently ideal nest-boxes in our gardens and find them rejected year after year, whereas other, to our eyes far less desirable, sites will be settled with alacrity and court almost inevitable disaster. That is one of the delights of watching garden birds, with their wild ways unsullied by our preconceptions.

Being Constructive

For most birds, the most agonising part of the nest-building process appears to be deciding upon the right site. The next stage, constructing the nest itself, can have the feel of an afterthought once the hard choices have been made. And many structures seem to reflect this. Pigeon nests can have such a slapdash foundation that it is possible to see the eggs from below. House Sparrows simply stuff material in a hole, giving their nests the unmistakable signature of a cowboy builder. Even the Robin, which builds quite a respectable model of leaves, grass, moss and finer materials, only takes about four days from start to finish, working just a few hours each day, mostly in the morning.

As mentioned above, nest-building is often a feminine discipline. Some females, indeed, become quite aggressive if the male should intrude upon their labour. But this doesn't mean that the males can relax for a few days. Apart from defending their territory, many spend this time acting as providers, bringing extra rations of food to their mates while the latter are working on the nest and forming the first egg inside them.

This mate feeding, or 'courtship-feeding', is a touching display of togetherness, as well as serving a useful purpose. A female Great Tit, for example, feeling peckish, will call softly to her mate, and he will land nearby with a juicy, caterpillar in his bill. Immediately the female will crouch down, open her mouth and flutter her wings, in an attitude closely reminiscent of the begging of a baby bird. The male delivers his gift without ceremony, and then both carry on with their respective tasks. It won't be long before the next time: the female may make up to fifty requests a day for these priceless food parcels.

Guard Duty

Another chivalrous practice that can take the place of courtship feeding is guard duty. This is where a male attends a feeding female and watches out for danger on her behalf. This is a surprisingly efficient way to ensure that she obtains the extra food she needs, since her foraging will be much less disturbed and much more nourishing than usual. In the course of normal life, a feeding bird must make many anxious glances upward to check for danger, but the guarding male eliminates the need for his partner to make these time-wasting lifts of the head.

In truth, chivalry is only part of it and the anxiously guarding male is not only watching out for danger. He is also on the lookout for rivals, and with good reason. This period, just before and during egg-laying, is when the female is most fertile and tempting, and when the intrusions of other males can do most damage to a bird's paternity. Males must not let their females out of their sight, not even for one moment.

Feral Pigeons have a special mate-guarding technique, known as driving. Aware of the flightiness of their hormonal females, males treat them brutally during their peak of fertility, turning the danger period into one long forced march.

Wherever a female walks, the male is hard on her heels, almost tripping on her tail, pecking her at intervals to keep her going. A female has no time to do anything except what she must – feed, preen, fly – in the presence of the overbearing male. It's not pretty, and it must be desperate at times for both sexes, but it obviously works.

Colonial Swallows have remarkably devious ways of keeping their females honest. In this species the fairer sex is notoriously indifferent to fidelity, and in the melee of a colony it's easy for any bird to slip away from the attentions of its jealous mates. But the distracted males don't sink into despair upon finding their females unleashed; they simply put out a public announcement that a dangerous predator is at hand. It's a lie, of course, but the whole colony responds to the drill in the usual way, flying as one above the nesting areas

The Nuthatch plasters its hole entrance with mud, to suit its own dimensions and nobody else's.

and bunching together. Quite naturally, Swallows in fear of their lives are not given to fornication, so the deceiving male achieves his aim of protecting his paternity. In addition, with the colony clustered, he can usually relocate his female easily enough. That this extraordinary technique of crying wolf has arisen – equivalent to a suspicious human partner setting off a fire alarm in a seedy motel – shows just how fragile the pair-bond can be in the lives of many birds.

Of course, this merely reflects the motto of every bird's breeding season – reproduce to your maximum. If a sexier, fitter specimen of either sex lives next door, many a bird will be lured into so-called 'extra-pair copulation'. Pair-bonds are often links of convenience, not of affection.

The Dawn Chorus

THE DAWN CHORUS begins by lapping at your toes, and ends up as total immersion. What starts as a lone voice in the darkness builds up, bit by bit, into a multitude of voices, all competing for attention, like the din from dealers on the floor of the Stock Exchange. A wave of sound forms in the twilight, gets stronger and stronger, crashes over, then subsides as the brighter light of the new day takes hold and banishes the shouts to whispers, and the babble to individual homily. In April it is over by half past five, and by then much business has been done.

The first strains of the new day are heard from a wakeful Blackbird or Robin, both of which have large eyes and can see well in the half-light. They are joined by other species in a particular order, always much the same in a certain location, but varying from place to place. Song Thrushes are always in the first round, stating each of their phrases several times, with slow, clear enunciation, and with a wild-sounding air. Sooner or later a Wren will intervene, blurting out its long, over-fast and indignantly loud sentence again and again, like a cornered politician. The Woodpigeon soothes matters with its rhythmic, five-note coo, throaty and deep, the alto to a company of sopranos. The Dunnock warbles unremarkably, the Great Tit chimes cheerfully and, always a little later, the Chaffinch utters an accelerating rattle with a flourish for a finish. If we heard such a racket from our human neighbours we would complain about the noise, and yet most of suburbia sleeps through this dawn din, unaware of the miracle on its doorstep.

Many Theories

But if the buzz outside should awaken us from our slumber, perhaps we might – not necessarily politely or appreciatively – pause to wonder at the purpose behind it? Even if we do understand the general reason for singing, we might still question why this outpouring of noise should be happening now, in the chilly half-light, when we would rather be asleep? What makes birds shout so loudly when the day hasn't yet started?

The answer, it seems, is as concealed as the vocalists themselves behind their darkened cloak

Many people think that the Great Spotted Woodpecker's rapid drumming sound is made by the bird excavating a hole: in fact, it is purely to sound a territorial beat, equivalent to a song.

of spring leaves. There are plenty of theories, but a definitive one has so far proven elusive. Currently, the different ideas compete among themselves for attention. But perhaps they all hold a degree of truth, each explaining a small piece of a wider puzzle? Nothing in the lives of our garden birds is entirely neat and simple, so why should this be?

We can quickly admit some meteorological evidence. It appears that, of all times of day, dawn is the best moment to be heard. It's a gentle time atmospherically, with reduced wind turbulence and close conditions, when sound echoes off an invisible ceiling of air a few metres above ground, keeping it locked in and easily heard. The dawn is also environmentally apposite. If you were to make a speech at dawn, it would transmit to your neighbourhood twenty times more efficiently than at midday, when the garden reverberates to the sound of cars, planes, children, lawnmowers, radios, workmen and thousands of other pollutants. It is an ideal time to make an impression.

At the same time, it's by no means an ideal time for feeding. Much as birds' tummies must rumble at dawn, when it's many hours since their last meal, searching for food may well prove unsuccessful. Birds usually hunt by sight, so the low lighting conditions make foraging difficult. At the same time, the relative cold renders invertebrates, the main spring food of our garden birds, as inactive as early-morning students after a night at a club. Being cold-blooded, the insects require warmth before they can emerge on to leaves and branches. What better a time for birds to put all their efforts into singing, a task that requires no light or warmth from the sun?

Song Thrushes get up early, and are one of the first contributors to the dawn chorus.

Birds can be food items, too, of course, and yet another theory of dawn singing is that it's a way of making a lot of noise without putting yourself at unacceptable risk from predators. Most things that eat birds require good light by which to hunt and those that don't, such as owls, could perhaps be expected to have full stomachs by dawn after a night of feeding. Singing, making a commotion from a prominent perch, is a potentially dangerous occupation whose threats may be contained by performing under cover of the semi-darkness.

But what of the birds' relationships to each other? We know that singing birds are in competition, so perhaps this holds another key to

the dawn dilemma? One possibility seems especially likely. The nights, even in April can be cold, and some birds, tragically overstretched or inopportunely diseased, expire overnight. Like a bunch of school kids answering the register, maybe birds sing at dawn to confirm their presence, to put up their hands and say 'I'm here'? If so, vacancies would quickly become apparent, and new occupants would then be rapidly and unceremoniously installed. So much for the discredited notion that birds sing when they are happy!

But the most intriguing explanation for the dawn chorus is also by far the sauciest. Drawn from studies of Great Tits, it contends that birds may sing during the earliest part of the day to keep their females out of mischief. In the Great Tit at least, and probably in the Blackbird too, the peak of the dawn chorus coincides with the females' fertile periods, the time when a male's paternity is potentially most at risk. Females lay their daily egg at dawn, and from this moment on are rabidly fertile. It is in a male's urgent interest that, as soon as the female comes off the nest, he is ready outside for her, singing loudly, and speaking the language of copulation. Once he succeeds in mating with her, his song output drops – one is tempted to suggest, in sheer relief. If he is absent from his post, she will be vulnerable to the charms and attentions of neighbouring males, and his paternity is compromised. In the Great Tit, then, the dawn chorus appears to be a form of mate-guarding.

Whatever theory you choose, the dawn chorus carries on. That's sometimes the beauty of the familiar. We all know it happens, and many good minds have been stretched to explain it, but it's still a mystery welling up from the apparently commonplace. When it wakes you next, though, spare a thought for the stressed-out mate-guarding Great Tit, and go back to sleep with your irritation soothed by a degree of suitable sympathy.

In Praise of Pigeons

PIGEONS HAVE AN image problem. They need a good publicist. While Robins can be rotten to each other and are universally adored, our pigeon species are largely inoffensive, yet often loathed. At best we find them boring; at worst we find them unacceptably greedy, so we try to shoo them from our bird tables. In the country they are shot, and in towns we try to get the council to eradicate them from our roofs. Even their pleasing, gentle songs are an irritant to the more highly strung sections of human society, probably the same sort of people who complain about cows and cockerels making too much din near their second homes. But the reality is that these underrated birds are gems. They should have an appreciation society formed for them.

The Garden Trio

We have three species of pigeons that regularly use our gardens. The best known species, the one that packs into town squares and urban streets, is probably best called the Feral Pigeon, a dolly-mixture species of many colours and patterns, each individual slightly different. It originated from a creature called the Rock Dove, which still exists in the wild in some far-flung parts of the world, such as Atlantic sea-cliffs and Saharan rock formations, but has been domesticated for many centuries. White doves, carrier pigeons, racing pigeons and fantail pigeons are all descended from Rock Doves, and the versions that have escaped from pigeon lofts and dovecotes to live wild on man-made cliffs and concrete formations are birds of great adaptability and purpose. Carrier pigeons have fed armies and saved lives. Racing pigeons contain enough information in their tiny brains to take them across continents with street-number accuracy. They are historically and scientifically remarkable. Yet we still despise them.

The Woodpigeon is the big pigeon with the white patch on either side of its neck, and with the permanently astonished expression. It always looks plump and healthy, and hence especially ill-deserving of the food we put out on our bird-tables. We see it everywhere, and know of its abundance. And it is, at various times according to vagaries of population, the

most numerous bird in the country. But the question is: do we love a successful species? If we were neutral we should really find no trouble admiring this serial winner of our farms and streets.

The smallest of the trio is the fawn-coloured Collared Dove (pigeons and doves are effectively the same thing). Of the three it has the longest tail and the slimmest frame and a signature black-and-white ring around

A Woodpigeon launches from a high perch on the first leg of its display-flight.

its neck. It looks the least offensive, yet it is as astonishing a bird colonist as our country has ever seen. In 1954 there were no Collared Doves in Britain at all, yet by the end of the last century, just under fifty years later, there were 200,000 pairs. They spread explosively, one moment absent in a location, the next abundant - a coup by coo, all under their own steam. Like the Feral

Pigeon, the Collared Dove has a hidden history.

These three characters, then, should really be appreciated more, and welcomed into the garden. They should be fed and pampered and spoken about over garden fences. People should write about them in local papers, as they do about Robins. Why not? They are just as interesting and involving as any other garden birds.

Even if it were not for their remarkable histories and capabilities, we could still indulge a regard for pigeons on sole account of their very pleasing flight-displays. From the milder days of midwinter to the sultry days of July, pigeons take to their air to announce their ownership of our roofs, trees or gardens. These carefully choreographed advertising flights are as much a part of enjoying the spring as seeing the first Swallow or delighting in the first bloom of crocus, and few bird displays are as easy to observe and enjoy. Each species follows a different aerial routine over and above the garden, making patterns in the sky. It's like one's own personal air-show, only cheaper and much quieter.

Feral Pigeons courting on the paving stones. In this pigeon species, most display takes place on the ground.

The Collared Dove launches its display from a rooftop or aerial, suddenly interrupting a bout of cooing to set off skywards and fly vertically with very fast and full flaps of its wings - so full in fact that they often make a clap or two. After a fast climb taking it up 10 m (30 ft) or so, it levels out, spreads its wings and tail, floats for a moment, then free-falls in a straight line or a gentle spiral. It lands upon the same or another high perch, utters a self-satisfied high-pitched purring (sounding a bit like a roll-up party trumpet) and looks around to challenge other males to do the same.

Slaps and Claps

Woodpigeons also take to the air during long periods of territorial cooing, as if they had suddenly grown tired of perch-bound proclamation and decided they needed a change. They set off from a tree and fly in a shallow arc upwards and straight ahead, like a plane taking off, their wing-beats increasing in speed until these, too, suddenly make sharp, slapping sounds. This is the signal for an instant stall, as if the performer had been shot by its very own wing-claps. With wings and tail spread, it begins to glide downwards again, accelerating towards the ground in a straight line. At an appropriate moment it flaps its wings again to level out and then, if the fancy takes it, it repeats its roller-coaster ride until the need to show off subsides.

A displaying Collared Dove hangs in the air before spiralling down to earth.

Feral Pigeons adopt a minimalist approach. They fly out from their nesting perches, on a window ledge or roof perhaps, and, in true pigeon style, clap their wings a few times. Thrilled by making such a sound, they then simply glide forward, with wings held upwards in a V, turn and come into land, perhaps adding a little flourish by rocking from side to side at the last moment. It's not a very impressive sight but, for Feral Pigeons, the real display business takes place on the ground. We've all seen it, in our local parks or on our roofs. A male sidles up to a female, ruffling his feathers and spreading his tail, uttering his stammering coo, bowing, circling around her to get her attention. As often as not the female treats this approach with indifferent disdain, eyeing him with a cold stare.

Pigeons are familiar, of course, and perhaps over-familiar, which is why we struggle to appreciate them. But why not play this game: watch the pigeons flying their routines above your garden, and give each one a mark for artistic merit every time they try, as if you were the judge at a skating contest? Some will make better wing-claps, some will make better spirals or better forward dives; you'll soon spot the difference between individual efforts. As you do so, you'll realise what an asset a pigeon is to a garden. And you'll never see a Robin performing a display like one of these.

Migrant Arrivals

IT'S EASY ENOUGH to watch the floral forward march of spring in the garden, as each flower comes out in its own time. Snowdrops pierce the January soil, crocuses cloak February lawns and daffodils cluster in March bunches like picnickers spread out over a sward of turf. It's also possible to tick off our resident birds' breeding progress, as species begin, one by one, to sing, build nests and hatch out their young. Yet there are few more wondrous or significant sets of spring milestones than the first arrivals of summer-visiting migrant birds. For their sheer effort, and for sheer determination, these miniature travellers deserve every frisson of delight that greets their coming.

The summer visitors have an order of appearance, albeit a somewhat informal one, prone to fluctuate with the feats of certain individuals. So, for example, the Chiffchaff is usually the first to be seen or heard in the spring, often in the third week of March, but it might well be pipped to the post by the exceptional endeavour of a particular Swallow. Nevertheless, a real delight of being a garden watcher is to salute each species turning up for its first day of term, year by year, comparing one season with another. It provides us with a comfort and a yardstick. Whatever disaster might befall us, the bird migrants will still come at about the same time, indifferent yet reassuring.

There is much behind their sequence of clocking-in, variable though it is. It's a clue to each bird's journey, and to what each expects to find when finally it arrives here. The bald dates hide a rich treasury of information.

Take the Chiffchaff and Willow Warbler. These are small, tit-sized, olive-green birds with thin bills that hunt restlessly for insects in newly open pussy-willows and other blossoms, darting from branch to branch with detached busyness and flicking their wings ceaselessly as if trying to relieve their pent-up energy. They only stay to breed in the largest gardens, but often turn up in unusual places on migration in the spring, even pocket-handkerchief sized plots with a handful of bushes. The Chiffchaff always arrives first, since it has the shortest journey, coming only from the Mediterranean region where it suns itself during the winter. The Willow Warbler is a 'proper' migrant, wintering in Africa and making the extended journey under power of its slightly longer wings. Impressively, it doesn't lag far behind its associate, arriving here in about the first week of April.

The aerial visitors stagger their arrival, not so much because of their respective journeys, but because of their differing food requirements when they get here. The Swallow arrives first, notwithstanding its exceptional journey from the southern tip of Africa. With its vanguard over our shores by the first week of April, it is more content than other aerial feeders to skim low down and make best use of the shelter-belts, and also to take advantage of a wide selection of prey. The House Martin and Swift, with slightly shorter journeys from tropical Africa, are fussier. Both are more dependent than the Swallow on the later seasonal build up of hordes of airborne insects. The House Martin eventually arrives at the end of the month, fluttering to and fro in narrow arcs at rooftop height or more. The Swift is later still, delaying its main appearance until the first week of May. It needs plenty of tiny aerial insects and spiders, food that is so small that the merest breath of wind can whisk it out of reach. These high fliers must wait until clear conditions and gentle winds allow the air to grow thick with food. As far as they're concerned it's no good arriving at a restaurant at six o'clock when it does not open until eight.

The Spotted Flycatcher arrives with sun on its back. It feeds on butterflies and bluebottles, large, dozy insects that make for a significant mouthful. A few arrive late in April, when cold rainy weather will make life difficult. These early adventurers will have to forage on the ground, something they detest doing. But most wait until May– even towards the end of the month – before they put in an appearance. Then the borders are abundant with large, showy flowers and their heavy insect traffic is drugged on nectar.

There are other migrants to look out for. The Blackcap is another species that usually arrives in April, singing its pleasing whistling song before perhaps moving on to a woodland edge. Later in the month, a Whitethroat might make an appearance, especially to gardens with plenty of brambles and nettles. Well blessed plots might have other visitors, too; Turtle Doves come to farmyards, Yellow Wagtails to meadows, Cuckoos to commons. Some stay to breed, some pass by, others you might see one day simply flying over, on their way to a distant location, casting only their shadow upon your hallowed turf. They might be casual visitors, but they should not be discounted. Every one marks the progress of spring.

Weather Problems

BIRDS DO WHAT they can to ensure breeding success. They try to obtain the best possible mate, try to build the best possible nest, and they give their all to the chicks. But whatever their efforts, the outcome isn't always in their hands. Predation may dash their intent, so might disease, or a serious outbreak of fleas, ticks or mites. And of course nothing affects the productivity of garden birds quite as much as the weather. The unreliable grip of climate afflicts the breeding season of every bird, from the early days of singing and nest-building, to the critical hours and days spent looking after eggs or chicks.

At first bad weather is a pain, but not a disaster. Birds may sing less in the cold, and nest construction might be impaired by wind or rain, but these are losses that can be made up for later. Once eggs have been laid or hatched, however, the mood changes. Then a few days of cold can be life-threatening, to both adults and chicks.

The greatest danger that bad weather brings is to compromise incubation or brooding. Any bird sitting on eggs or chicks has a sober duty to them, but also has to survive itself. So at some point during prolonged cold or wet weather, a parent must go to feed, even if it means leaving the brood exposed (in most small birds, incubation is not shared by the sexes). This of course, could be lethal, but, sadly, the parent bird has little choice.

What makes this worse is that bad weather also affects the food supply. In cold weather many invertebrates become far less active than usual, making them harder to find in the numbers required. And in the rain or wind, searching can be made more difficult because of the movement of the leaves. If the showers are prolonged the water may literally wash vast quantities of insects from the trees on to the ground, where they are harder to find. Each of these problems makes the search for food longer, and the danger to the brood greater.

Of course, once they are out of the nest, the young birds find these difficulties transferred to them. Being new to the task of finding food for themselves, fledglings will be affected more than most if the rain makes caterpillars or other insects harder to detect among the shaking leaves. Much rain in late May and early June inevitably causes high losses among fledgling tits and Chaffinches.

But it's not only cold and rainy weather that creates a problem. For example, too much warmth may cause caterpillars (on which tits especially rely) to develop and pupate more quickly than usual, so that there are not so many around later in the season when the young birds leave the nest. And drought, too, carries its problems. Again the caterpillar supply will be badly affected, leaving numbers depleted.

However, other birds actually benefit from a wet spring, so long as the rain is not excessive. Blackbirds and Song Thrushes need mud for their nests and worms for their nestlings. In a drought both are in short supply: the mud will be dry earth, and the earthworms will be protected by the hard ground. They need a good sprinkling of rain.

The weather cannot please everybody all the time but, whatever its tendencies, birds will be affected in some way, good or bad. The best spring of all will be warm with a generous but patchy supply of rain, but that happens only occasionally. Every other spring brings its meteorological mixture of blessing and peril.

A quick April shower won't bother the nesting Song Thrush, but prolonged periods of rain can bring disaster.

IT'S MAY AND, for the first time in the year, the skies fill up with professional insect-catchers. Squadrons of newly-arrived Swifts, definitive fair-weather birds, wheel around the rooftops and scream their approval at arriving upon their breeding grounds after the long winter away. Whizzing between chimneys and making circuits around the neighbourhood, they bring to mind groups of teenagers tearing around the streets in fast cars, finally unleashed from their childhood.

MAY

New Arrivals

IT'S THE FIFTH month of the year, and the garden is bursting with new growth and busy lives. The daffodils have been whisked unceremoniously from the borders, to be replaced by bluebells, primulas, grape-hyacinths and a host of other showy plants. Leaves barge out from their buds one by one and put a collective veil over the inner workings of trees and shrubs, keeping the lives of the secretive birds, like the skulking Wren, hidden from sight. The resident birds are zipping back and forth from their recently constructed nests with bills stuffed with tiny bodies to nourish other tiny bodies. And now, with the migration season well advanced, the summer visitors are here to inflict further toll on the garden's hard-pressed invertebrate life.

The arrival of these summer migrants – Swift, Swallows, martins, flycatchers and warblers – is often described as a "changing of the guard" in the garden, and yet it is not quite like that. The well installed resident birds have no intention of making space for any incoming upstarts; new arrivals must squeeze into places where they can. No matter; the immigrants would not be immigrants if they shared exactly the same niches as those already here. Somehow the garden, and its burgeoning resources, can hold them all.

But these latecomers have much catching up to do, and no time to rest. They are crammers, taking five months to do what others may do in seven or eight. Their lives are full of quick decisions and cut corners.

The males of these migrants arrive on site first, breathless from their travels, a week or so before their potential mates and long enough to sort themselves out and fit into hastily defined territories. Pair-formation then takes place with almost indecorous speed, usually within a few days, and it's difficult not to conclude that the hurried potential partners must take a look, declare 'You'll do' in a snap decision, and entrust their season to a stranger. In reality, many will opt for their mate of the previous year, and the rest will make some kind of external assessment. But the couple have barely enough time to get acquainted before they find themselves nest-building, laying eggs and catching up with the tail-enders among the resident breeding species. This is Ready Steady Breed, the fast version of procreation.

The outcome of the migrants' fast-track approach is that the majority of garden birds will be well into breeding routine by the middle of the month, whether they have been here since the chilly days of January or have arrived at some point in the last week or two. And whatever their precise timetables, one thing will unite every one of them at some stage in the calendar month of May: all, at one time or another, will be sitting on eggs.

While nest-building can be almost a relaxed - or at least brief - affair, the production of eggs puts considerable stress upon every female of every species. An egg is large – weighing up to a fifth of a bird's own body weight – and it is burdensome, too, in the resources diverted to it. An egg-laying female must be a well-fed female, and she must be selective in her foraging as well. Eggshells, for example, require calcium for their formation, an element that is not at all easy to find in the garden, except in the shells of tiny snails.

Most bird species lay several eggs, but they always stagger their production, laying one egg a day for as many days as it takes to complete their allotted clutch. The reason for this is simple: if a bird had to carry a set of fully formed eggs, it

Previous Page: *Swifts breed in colonies, and their communal fits of squealing are a sign that they are intending to stick together.*

Left: *As summer visitors like the Willow Warbler arrive in force, new voices increase the intensity and diversity of the dawn chorus.*

would be unable to take off. So, although it will have several eggs developing at any one time, one is always well in advance of the rest. Most birds go to roost in a heavily pregnant state and lay at dawn - an early delivery, if you like, of a wrapped-up parcel. This leaves them relatively unencumbered during the feeding part of the day.

How many eggs are laid by each individual bird, and by each species varies a great deal. Naturally there are general trends; House Sparrows, which normally lay four or five eggs, don't suddenly wake up one morning and decide that their clutch will be fifty, carried away on a whim of overproduction. Natural selection sets the limits, based on what has been successful during the ancestry of the species. But recent research on Great Tits has shown that the size of the clutch also appears to be an inherited trait.

Heavy Burdens

Even so, some garden birds lay so many eggs that it must be a huge burden to look after them all. The lot of a Blackbird or Robin, with typically four or five eggs per brood, seems bad enough. But a woodpecker may lay seven, a Pheasant or Mallard ten and a tit, the quintessential over-producer, will regularly lay into the teens. The record for a Great Tit is actually twenty-four - but one might assume that such an overambitious family line died out!

Some birds, including Swallows and Starlings increase their output by donating eggs to other parents of the same species, a trick with the grand name of 'intraspecific brood parasitism'. A female completes her own clutch but, like every bird, wishes to maximise her productivity as an individual. So she steals into the nest of a neighbour while they're not looking, and, Cuckoo-like, lays an egg. If the chick hatches it will be raised by foster-parents and this, for the donating parents, constitutes productivity with minimum effort. So cost-effective is the practice of intraspecific brood parasitism that it is surprising that so few species appear to do it. But perhaps more will be discovered in the future.

Of course, all these eggs must be fertilised,

The late arriving Spotted Flycatcher crams its whole breeding cycle into a few short, hard-working weeks.

whatever their origin, and that's achieved by the act of copulation. The majority of male birds don't have a penis, but an external opening, the cloaca, through which sperm can be ejected. Copulation is achieved simply by contact between the cloaca of the male and that of the female. A male bird mounts, both sexes twitch their tail to the side, their cloacae touch for a second or so, and that's that. Considering that copulation is so pivotal to reproduction, it is achieved with almost unseemly haste.

But what birds lack in quality, they certainly make up for in quantity. Many species copulate repeatedly throughout the nest-building and egg-laying period. A Robin, for example, has been observed to copulate two and a half times an hour over 195 hours of surveillance and it is reasonable to assume that many species do much the same. Their hard toil is necessary, from both viewpoints: for a female it ensures that each egg will be safely fertilised; for a male repeated copulation safeguards his paternity.

The male is wise to flood his mate with sperm as often as possible. The act of mating, as we've seen, is quick and easy, and open to instantaneous abuse. At the same time, a female's fertile period lasts for at least two weeks, providing an extended window of opportunity for loitering males, of which there are always plenty around, even in a garden. As a result extra-pair liaisons appear to be commonplace. So the more a male copulates with his partner in such a permissive environment, the more he will be able to dilute any unwelcome sperm.

A male Dunnock doesn't settle for dilution. Should he lose sight of his mate and become suspicious about her

The tender and prolonged courtship between two feral pigeons culminates in a brief and undignified flurry of wings as they mate.

recent activities, he initiates sexual activity as soon as he comes across her again. After a short period of stimulation he makes for her cloaca, and unromantically gives it a sharp peck. Out slips any offending sperm, like a coin from a slot machine. His paternity is preserved – for the moment.

Colonies are short on privacy, even for these most intimate of acts, and Rooks appear to be especially prone to red-faced misunderstandings over copulation. The inciting display of a female, her invitation to mate, usually takes place upon the nest, and merely consists of the bird drooping her wings and lowering her head. It doesn't look very different from her normal posture when incubating the eggs, and for this reason, or perhaps simply opportunism, male Rooks constantly pester sitting females and attempt to copulate with them, often several times a day. These 'attempted rapes' invariably cause outrage among neighbouring males, which step in to interrupt the proceedings, attacking both male and female. Yet even the interventionists themselves may be overcome by

temptation, trying out what they had originally come to impede. So in Rook society, as in many other species' societies, it is often a matter of guesswork as to who exactly is responsible for the genetic contents of each egg.

Clutch Control

That said, the female, smug in the knowledge that the eggs are her handiwork at least, must now settle down to the next part of the breeding cycle, incubation. Contrary to popular belief, incubation usually starts only when the clutch is complete, not as soon as the first egg is laid. In Blackbirds it begins five days after the first egg is laid and in tits as much as ten days afterwards. When an egg is laid the development of the embryo, so fast and intense inside the female's body, is halted; only when incubation begins will it accelerate again. By leaving incubation until the last (or often, the second-last) egg is laid, a parent ensures that all the eggs will hatch within a day or two of each other, making feeding the brood logistically easier, and giving each chick, theoretically at least, an equal chance of survival.

It doesn't always work like this. A few birds in the garden, including Swifts, operate a quite different incubation strategy. They begin with the first egg, and lay their eggs more than a day apart. The inevitable result is a brood of chicks – sometimes two, occasionally three – all of different ages. Although it doesn't know it, the first chick is its parents' insurance policy: as the eldest it gets the first offerings of food, eats greedily and has an excellent chance of survival. The second chick is a bonus. Its turn comes to be fed when its elder sibling is satisfied, so it will survive if food is plentiful and its sibling is serially satiated. A third chick is a perk, last in line, a share option for an exceptional summer.

May, then, sees waves of new arrivals, from the turning up of late migrants to the hatching of chicks everywhere. The population of birds in the garden has increased greatly in recent weeks. From now on, though, the trend will be downward. Instead of gains in the garden there will be huge losses. Eggs and chicks are vulnerable, and parenting is a daunting challenge. Many trials await those embroiled in it.

Shocking Tactics Among Swallows

RECENT STUDIES ON birds have thrown up some unpalatable truths. Where we once thought that most birds were faithful to their partners, we now know that the majority are not. When once we thought that birds sang for pleasure, we now know that song is stressful and carries a message of threat. Where once we thought that birds lived in peace, now we know that violence and discord are never far away. Sometimes knowledge can be a double-edged sword, jolting us from comfortable preconceptions.

And no bird's reputation has been so badly damaged by scrutiny as that of the Swallow. Revered as a harbinger of spring, adored for its association with us and our buildings, and admired as an attractive-looking bird with a pleasing song, it has long been one of our most popular birds. But now some highly unpleasant revelations threaten that popularity, as you will see.

The Swallow, it transpires, plays exceptionally dirty in the breeding season. For a start it is highly promiscuous. Swallows pair with one mate in a formal relationship, but that's a bit of a sham: both sexes waste no chance to copulate with many of their neighbours. When a male's mate is incubating he has time to seek out other females and increase his genetic influence. And while the male is away from the nest feeding, the female becomes accustomed to visits from various suitors. If they are more desirable than her mate, with longer and more symmetrical tails, for instance, she will have no hesitation in making their visits well worthwhile. Many a female will

mate with almost all of her nearest neighbours.

Such nest-hopping is not particularly unusual among birds. It's almost standard procedure. However, events take a far more sinister and unusual turn among Swallows when individual males find themselves still unpaired well into the breeding season, a situation they find completely unacceptable. In this rarefied situation, tactics become extreme.

Soft Targets

This is where murder enters the scene. One might expect a male bird to kill another male whose mate he desires, but that carries too much risk to the potential assailant. Instead he picks upon the softest of soft targets, the newly hatched young. Swallows, you see, sometimes commit infanticide.

It's all too simple really. An unpaired male will watch and wait to see how young families are faring. He will know who is paired with whom, how well they are relating, and whether divorce is likely. He will know which pairs have eggs, and how long before they hatch. He will be the first to find out when a bird is widowed and vulnerable. Above all he will be very clear which females are the most desirable. In summary, he is

It's easy for a Swallow to kill another pair's brood. It simply picks the youngsters up in its bill one by one, and drops them over the side of the nest.

a malign influence awaiting his chance.

The unpaired male given to infanticide will strike when the chicks of a desirable female have only just hatched. The opportunity will come when both parents are away from the nest for whatever reason, perhaps feeding or drinking, or even having a liaison with a member of the opposite sex. He will fly to the nest, pick up a helpless chick in his bill, and simply dump it over the side. The members of the brood are thrown out one by one. Their demise is not instantaneous but it is inevitable, because the parents cannot and will not make any attempt to retrieve them. The deed is done.

The parents are faced with ruin when they return, for in a few moments of carelessness, everything they have invested in the breeding attempt has come to nought. They are now certain to divorce. The male has failed in his responsibility to protect the nest and its contents, and the female summarily rejects him.

Since this now leaves a female with no mate and only a short time left to breed, she will quickly enter into a fast-track hunt for a replacement. Any number of males might fit the bill but, in terms of expedience, which one do you think might be in pole position? Not surprisingly, the liquidator of her own chicks is ready and waiting. It is common for the male that carried out the infanticide to pair and reproduce with the female that was the victim of his spoiling. It's even possible that she might be aware of it. But such is the need to breed that the male with blood on his beak enters into the respectability of pairing and parenting.

It is not only males that have spent the early season unpaired that are prepared to kill the chicks of a rival. Sometimes an individual finds himself unexpectedly without a mate mid-season due to death or desertion, and makes good his loss in the same unpleasant way. And widowed females are at particular risk. If they have young in the nest, it is highly unlikely that a new mate would be so magnanimous as to help her raise the offspring of her deceased partner. Again, unfortunately, the nestlings pay the price.

It would be wrong to assume that infanticide was a common tactic among Swallows. In one very thorough study of a large colony it occurred in only fourteen of 298 broods. But reputations are made by deeds, not percentages, and there is no doubt that the Swallow, such a popular spring herald, now risks being lambasted in people's hearts and minds for its very extreme version of promoting paternity.

Diary of an Outcast – The Cuckoo's Story

CUCKOOS AREN'T CAPABLE of cognitive thought, as far as we know, and they certainly don't write diaries. But garden birdwatchers can do both, and are also able to indulge in flights of fantasy. This is the excuse, then, for the following narrative, detailing the spring activities of an adult female Cuckoo: the Diary of an Outcast.

First Week of May

I've arrived at last. It's been a long journey from Africa, taking several weeks. It's good to be back. There are just as many beetles and caterpillars around as last year, which means that I will be ready to get my breeding programme underway soon.

It's also heartening to hear quite a few males singing; in fact, one was singing well at dawn when I got to the rough ground where I shall hold territory.

Second Week of May

I've spent most of the week asserting my own rights to this patch of ground, making sure that no other females are loitering inside. We females are the true territory-holders of our kind; our males are flexible about their borders. And within our patches we make sure we have several hosts of our foster species. Humans call our private domains 'egg territories'.

Caught in the act – a female Cuckoo about to lay in the nest of a foster parent, having removed the egg of the host.

The rest of the time I've been spending birdwatching. To be an effective brood parasite I have to know exactly what is going on among my host species. I perch in a concealed position and observe their comings and goings, undercover. I will be ready to intervene when they have begun to lay eggs.

Third week of May

I know the Dunnocks have started laying because of the female's secretive behaviour at dawn. I shall have to act soon. I need to make contact with one of the local male Cuckoos.

I soon have an approach from a male that hears me calling him. I'm pleased with my suitor because he's the very vigorous bird that dominates the neighbourhood with his cuckooing. We don't need many preliminaries, just a quick chase and it's over. He will have mated with lots of other females, and I might meet up with him again or I might not. It depends on whether our paths cross.

I did not find the Dunnock's nest, so I decided to try that little trick we Cuckoos have. Dunnocks are a bit thick, and this ruse pays dividends every time. It works on the principle of the 'warmer, colder' game. I approach the birds in broad daylight and know that they're going to react to me somehow. If they are only slightly disturbed I assume that I am some way from the nest, but if they go wild I know I'm close. I can gauge where the nest is from their reaction. I soon spot it, and I shall act tomorrow.

* * *

I didn't need to be up early. In fact, in mid-morning I have an approach from another male and, for variety's sake, I mate with him. The Dunnocks, meanwhile, have another egg, laid at dawn. I shall wait for my chance this afternoon.

Not many birds lay eggs in the afternoon, but that gives me the best chance of a successful infiltration. I watch the Dunnocks for hours, and eventually one - and then the other - leaves the nest. I shall have to act quickly now. I rush in as fast as I can without making myself too obvious. The path to the nest is a bit cramped through the branches of the bush, but I'm too excited to be put off. After so many hours of watching a nest, it feels a bit odd to be there. I sit on the rim and

Unseen by its parents or its foster-parents, the young Cuckoo eliminates the competition.

take one of the Dunnocks' eggs in my bill. I swallow it. Then, settling down, I lay my egg; it looks satisfyingly similar to the Dunnock one, good enough to dupe the parents anyway, but I have no time to admire it and must dash away. If I'm discovered my fosterers may desert. My visit to the Dunnock nest has taken only ten or fifteen seconds.

Fourth Week of May

My efforts are not finished yet. I have plenty of other Dunnocks on my patch and I have the same plans for them. I will try to lay ten eggs this year, but I know some female Cuckoos that have laid twenty.

You might ask why I choose Dunnocks. It's simple. I came out of a Dunnock's nest, and so I lay in Dunnocks' nests. It's obviously a family thing, because I know other Cuckoos select other species. A female down the road specialises in Robins, as will all the female nestlings of her parentage.

I was concerned today to catch sight of a female Cuckoo I didn't recognise, and on my own territory, too. While most of us are responsible and look after our own egg-territories, occasionally interlopers just come in and lay in our selected nests. Sometimes, infuriatingly, we come across a nest and find it is already parasitised. We still lay there, though, and expect a battle royal between our respective progeny.

I can see that the Dunnocks have accepted my egg. It's just as well, because if they had rejected it, I might have been forced to cause them to desert and start all over again – anything to make my fostering plans succeed. Now it's just a matter of waiting.

First Week of June

Although I cannot see it happening, I know that my first egg must have hatched. The egg developed a little in my oviduct, so it will win the race to hatch first, ahead of the Dunnock's eggs, taking twelve days in all. Once out of its shell, my chick will rest before starting to work hard to manipulate each Dunnock egg on to the small of its back and heave it over the side of the nest. It pays to eliminate the competition. Attaboy!

The males are still singing, just the same variety of good 'cuckoos' and hoarse 'cuckoos' that they sang earlier on. They don't change their tune in June at all. I have pretty much finished with my mating efforts, even though I have only laid nine eggs. The Dunnock nests proved pretty hard to find.

Second Week of June

I know it's rare, if not unknown for a Cuckoo to meet her own offspring, but I passed a juvenile in my egg territory this morning. It was making a fine job of opening its huge gape and begging loudly, imploring its foster parents to come

and feed it; in fact, it was so noisy it had visits from several of other species, all in a queue to stuff caterpillars down its gullet. It's doing well.

I had a rare moment of sociability later on. A male had discovered a glut of caterpillars on some nearby nettles, and several of us took the opportunity to gorge ourselves. No Cuckoo worries about rights to food like this. We're all far more concerned with egg territories and reproduction.

My role as a nest parasite has come to an end for the year. I will hang around for a few weeks, feeding to get into shape for my migration in August, avoiding the attentions of any angry birds that might wish to mob me. But few will notice my departure, and no human knows where precisely I spend my winter in Africa. In fact, humans hardly ever notice me at all – they only see the loudmouthed males when they're singing in the spring.

And hopefully the Dunnocks never notice me either. Until it's too late.

A Cuckoo's season approaches success: a youngster is out of the nest and is being well looked after.

A Helping Hand

ANYONE WHO STUDIES the garden soap opera in spring can hardly fail to notice that breeding birds are not, on the whole, co-operative. Individuals rarely help each other; on the contrary they are in competition and, as we've seen with Swallows, the demise of one can be an opportunity for another. The rule of competitiveness shouts out and makes its voice resoundingly clear.

However, there are a few exceptions. Most of them concern parents and their young, with the latter helping out the former. Among Swallows, and possibly House Martins too, there is a tradition for members of the season's first brood occasionally to help their parents feed the young of the second or third. They are being responsible kids, assisting with the task of aiding their siblings and giving them a good start in life. On ponds and rivers throughout the country, junior Moorhens do the same.

But the most outstanding case of mutual co-operation is found among blood relatives of the Long-tailed Tit. This, indeed, is one of the most sociable of birds. Individuals club together in flocks during the autumn, and all the members defend a group territory. Relationships between them are close because the flock is based on a single pair and its progeny from the previous breeding season. Over the course of the winter the males remain with their parents in the flock, while the female youngsters leave to join a neighbouring group, and they are replaced by unrelated females from outside. So the makeup of the flock changes during the winter. When spring comes the flock splits up amicably, each brother and partner occupying its own bit of the previously jointly held territory and making a nesting attempt.

Many of these nesting attempts fail; it's a fact of life. If the failure is total, and a renewed attempt is out of the question because of the lateness of the season, then the members of the pair will do a most unusual thing: they will assist at the nest of one of their siblings, playing their part in helping to feed the young. They don't go as a couple. The failure of the breeding attempt splits up the pair, because their responsibilities now lie purely towards their blood relatives. So the male goes to assist his blood relative and the female hers; they will help at different nests.

Although their own breeding attempt has failed, the helpers' presence at the nest of a sibling has a dramatic effect on the survival of the fortunate young – their

House Martins gather to collect mud, which they use to construct their neat under-eaves nest cups.

These young Long-tailed Tits have at least three adults attending to their needs, but some fortunate broods have as many as ten!

nephews and nieces. The amount of food brought in is greatly enhanced, and the pressure on the true parents is thus reduced, enabling them to stay in better condition. The arrangement may have its origins in disaster, but it is highly effective in increasing breeding success. Studies have shown that a nest may have more than one helper. There are often two, and one lucky pair is on record as having eight. With so many birds helping out, that nest in particular had no excuse not to prosper.

What of the helpers, though, those birds that are selflessly assisting their sibling? With their own chances of breeding gone that year, do they benefit in any way? The answer is a resounding 'yes'. As registered nest helpers, they have now qualified to join their brother's winter flock. As we shall see later in the year, membership of a flock has high survival value, and it is not conferred lightly.

So, in a world of competition, at least one bird stands out as different. The Long-tailed Tit is the only species in Britain to practise such a high level of mutual co-operation when it is breeding, although quite a few tropical birds have similar arrangements. And the most interesting feature is that absolutely everybody benefits. It's a beacon to every other bird in the garden. Sometimes a little co-operation goes a long way.

IT IS THE height of the breeding season, when all the paranoia of the last few months, over getting a territory and a mate, and then holding on to what you have gained, has at last dissipated with the chipping of the eggs in the nest. It's now far too late to worry about the parentage of your hatching chicks.

JUNE

The Parent Trap

FOR BIRDS, JUNE days are long in every sense. Many individuals are now parents, so hard work takes over as the main concern, with birds labouring throughout the extended hours of daylight, deep into what is at most seasons the night.

Parenting, of course, actually begins with the egg. It's easy to think of eggs as passive structures, or nameless packages, nothing more than glorified pebbles. But eggs have personality. Well before they hatch the embryos inside can hear the calls of their parents, and learn them. And before their shells break, these little proto-chicks can make their own sounds, cheeping back to their parents or even to their peers. One can imagine them saying to one another: 'Let's break out now, everybody!' in the close confinement of the nest.

Incubating eggs is not a passive process, either. The sitting bird doesn't just sit. He or she – and it is usually the female – continually turns the eggs over with her bill, so that every part of every egg is properly heated, just as one might turn a joint of meat roasting in the oven. And at surprisingly frequent intervals, the duty incubator takes a break. Female tits have breaks every fifteen minutes or so, leaving the nest for a five-minute foraging trip and a stretching of legs and wings.

Precisely how long a bird must incubate depends on the species of bird. However, for a diverse range of garden birds, from Blackbirds to tits and from Swallows to House Sparrows, incubation lasts about two weeks. Even larger birds like Carrion Crows take only slightly longer. This is no coincidence, for they all have a similar way of bringing up their young, as if they were all following the same guidebook, a Doctor Spock or a Contented Little Baby Bird Book.

We are so used to the image of helpless chicks in a nest, fed by their overworked and devoted parents, that we assume that every bird brings up

Previous page: *A Green Woodpecker feeds ants to its growing young.*

Below: *Chicks are a sign of success, but they demand hard work. This Pied Wagtail must bring food in several hundred times a day.*

It all looks peaceful now, but these young Blue Tits will start competing with each other as soon as the parents bring food.

its young this way. It doesn't. Chicks hatch with very different profiles. Several important groups of birds, including waterfowl such as Mallards or game birds such as Pheasants produce well-developed, highly mobile youngsters, the cute babies that our children love, the ducklings and goslings, and the fluffy chicks from hens. These are super-chicks, covered with down, eyes open and ready to run almost from the moment they hatch; they follow their mother but they can feed for themselves. In scientific parlance they are called precocial, although we might equally call them precocious. They hatch out prepared to meet their world. Their state of advancement is due to a longer development inside the egg, an extended incubation period.

But most of our garden birds, warmed under the adults for just two weeks, hatch in a very different state. They are naked, blind, and utterly nest-bound; they could not run for a centimetre. Sometimes we find them on our garden lawns or walkways after a raid by a predator. Tiny, pathetic,

and rather hideous, they are more like reptiles than birds. They cannot feed or warm themselves, and are completely dependent on their parents for all the basics of life. The scientists describe them as altricial; a parent bird, if it could do so, would describe them as hard work. Their most prominent features are a large head and a huge gape, which opens to reveal bright colours. These baby birds are mouths with bodies attached, designed to send their parents into a state of slavery.

Broken Eggshells

In their very first hours the hatchlings are dealt with tenderly. The adult female may assist with the final stages of hatching out, teasing any small bodies away from the shells that protected them. Any broken eggshells round about will then be removed quickly and taken out of the nest, enabling the female to crouch down to brood, heating her newborns with the warmth of the naked skin of her brood-patch. The chicks initially rely on yolk reserves for their nutriment, but it is not long before they are furnished with their first meal; water and earthworms for Blackbirds, the tiniest of caterpillars for Blue Tits. They are built to grow, and do so rapidly.

It's tempting to think that the subsequent scene around the nest, with the earnest mother incubating, the devoted male providing food and the frail chicks begging for their share, is one of harmony and mutual encouragement. But it isn't. Within hours of their life-out-of-eggshells starting, the chicks have launched into a state of cut-throat

This young Robin will have been fed an early diet of soft-bodied worms and caterpillars.

competition. Every time a parent arrives to offer food, there is something of a scrum, with each nestling reaching up as high as it can to catch its provider's attention, much as schoolchildren put up their hands with unusual vigour when offered sweets. The chick that thrusts its bill highest wins, and takes its first step towards survival. The rest must wait their turn. Already they have entered into a world of winners and losers.

In truth, it probably sounds more frantic than it usually is. It does not take much to satisfy a single chick. Studies on tits have shown that two small caterpillars will fill up a chick to the point where it must doze off and start digesting its meals. While it is sleeping its siblings can be fed, one by one, from the biggest to the smallest, until, we hope, each has obtained what it needs. The problem arises if food is hard to come by, either during a bad season or on a day of poor weather. In these circumstances the biggest and most vigorous chick might wake up and beg strongly before all its siblings have been fed. Then the

weakest may miss out several turns, and grow progressively less able to beg. It will soon fade away unless conditions outside rapidly improve.

We'll never know whether birds worry about the state of their chicks' health, or if they suffer stress if a particular individual dies. All we do know is that, from the very beginning, most parents keenly devote themselves to providing all the food that they possibly can to help their young survive. From dawn to dusk, even in the protracted daylight of June, they search high and low for suitable nourishment. For a pair of Blue Tits, with up to fourteen young in the nest, this will entail no fewer than five hundred excursions each, every day, for at least nineteen days.

The number of feeding trips depends on the type of food being brought in. The seemingly unbearable workload of tits stems from their habit of bringing in only one package at a time, enough to feed just one nestling one meal. The staple diet of both adults and young consists of caterpillars, and it seems that they bring one at a time in order to process them for their chicks' tender mouths. Caterpillars, you see, have jaws; they are leaf-munching machines. The jaw must be broken, and any other unpleasant body parts removed, before the offering is made to its tender recipient.

The burden for Blackbirds is different. Their young are fed mainly on soft-bodied worms, and these inoffensive meals can be delivered in bulk. So can the smallest insects. House Martins and Swifts feed their young on flying waifs as small and as easily squashed as aphids. Swift parents make only intermittent visits to their nestlings, but every one may yield over a thousand small meals, enough to keep the most demanding chick satisfied.

Food Shortage

In fact the bulk-delivering Swift is beset by potential problems during its chick-rearing period. Swift food is not fast food; it cannot be guaranteed all the time. And whilst other birds face difficulties every so often in providing food to their young, Swifts do so as a matter of course, since aphids and other tiny invertebrates float high above the garden in plankton-like clouds, making them very difficult to collect in large numbers unless the weather is fine and still. And as often as not, it isn't. The solution to the problem lies with the young. They build up fat reserves in their bodies when food is plentiful, becoming bloated and hardly Swift-like. Then, when shortages come, they use up their body fat and may decrease in weight by as much as a half. At the same time, if it's especially cold, they enter into a semi-torpid state, reducing their metabolic rate to save energy. All in all, young Swifts have a remarkable inbuilt resistance to starvation, bred in over the millennia of unpredictable supply.

Very few nestlings are designed to cope with food shortages or unpredictable provision like this. Starvation is the single biggest cause of death among nestlings, and happens in every garden every year, probably in almost every nest. We humans should not let ourselves become too distressed by this, even in these days when we can witness the whole tortuous outcome on our video cams. Young birds have for ever been over-produced. Even of those that manage to leave the nest, very few will survive to breed and bring up their own young. Among our common small birds, perhaps less than ten per cent of eggs will grow up to become adult members of the breeding population.

That doesn't stop the parents doing all they can to help them. And, besides the most obvious duty of bringing in the food, they have other responsibilities too. If starvation is the most serious threat to the young, disease and pest infestation are not far behind. The sanitation of the nest is an important and often overlooked task.

If environmental health officers were to visit the nest of a bird, they would probably pick out two main threats to hygiene: the faeces of the youngsters, and any nestlings that have died. The latter present the simplest, if not always satisfactory solution; those that can be removed are taken away by the parents, and those that cannot are left to rot and are trampled down by the

surviving nestlings. As for the deposits of the chicks, these are made as rather neat, white jelly-like packages known as faecal sacs. When a parent brings in food it will sometimes linger on the rim of the nest, waiting for a nestling to go bottom up. This is the sign for a faecal sac to be produced. The chick does what it must and the adult takes the white blob away in its bill, sometimes dropping it some distance away but at other times, particularly when the nestlings are very young, swallowing it. This may sound revolting, but young at an especially tender

Small success stories – these young Treecreepers have already come a long way, and will soon leave the nest.

age don't digest all their food particularly well, so the adults, if you like, finish their meals for them.

The Alien World

In their brief nestling existence baby birds undergo some remarkable changes very quickly. They increase their weight as much as tenfold, they grow a set of feathers, and they compete with their siblings for their very existence. From feeble beginnings, cold and naked in the bowels of the nest, the winners soon reach the size and weight of their parents. They engulf the nest platforms that once dwarfed them, or they fill up what was once a spacious hole. In the days prior to their departure, hole-nesting chicks attain such a state of vigour that they can reach up to the entrance and peer outside, getting their first taste of the alien world that awaits them.

It often takes a bit of encouragement to coax a well-grown chick from a nest and, as ever, the conscientious parents play a prominent role. Still in the habit of bringing food to their young, they present it but withhold it, so to speak, offering it pertinently just a little outside the nest. Hunger wins and the young bird launches itself on to an unsteady perch, to be quickly rewarded with the meal that was successfully used as bait.

House Martins are less subtle than most other garden birds about enticing their young from the nest. They have a special luring display, which is repeated over the course of several days. One or other parent will fly up to the nest repeatedly, hovering in front and offering calls of encouragement whilst the young remain resolutely attached to their mud-brick homes, like militant squatters unwilling to leave. Eventually, the female parent, perhaps exasperated, actually lands at the nest entrance. She doesn't provide any food at all, but apparently gives the chicks a mouthful of a different kind! This usually does the trick, and the mother flies off with a chastised youngster a few metres behind.

Occasionally among these sociable birds, the whole colony takes a hand in tempting broods, especially late ones, from their nests. Up to thirty

It's hard to learn how to hunt in the darkness, so this owlet will be dependent on its parents long after it is fully-feathered.

birds may fly excitedly around, going back and forth from the occupied dwellings, calling urgently and enticing the stay-at-homes to leave.

But very few birds are so public, for a very good reason. Leaving the nest is highly dangerous in itself, and the world outside is full of peril. Most broods fledge at dawn, under the concealment of the early morning. Their first day will be a dangerous and challenging one, and there is a good chance that many will not see it through to the end.

Are Magpies Bad?

IF YOU ARE reading this book, you probably already have an opinion on the matter of Magpies. Magpies polarise opinion, black or white. If you're on the black side, you may want to have them culled – or even to get rid of them yourself. If you're white, you probably harbour a secret admiration for them. If you're in the latter camp, confess it only in your own home, with the door locked.

Magpies excite a remarkable degree of hatred and to an extent it is earned. They are regular killers of the eggs and chicks of some small birds in the garden. They appear to go about their grim business with a certain ruthlessness, and frequently perform their worst in front of horrified householders' eyes. Gardens with resident Magpies can appear to have a lower population of birds than gardens without, and the impression gained is that they terrorise the smaller birds into going elsewhere, either in the breeding season or during the winter. If this observation is true then they must be a widespread menace, in part responsible for the widely perceived – and largely real – reduction in small bird populations over the last ten or twenty years. That is the case for the prosecution.

In defending the Magpie, one must first hear its confession with an open mind. This is an open and shut case, with only mitigation, not acquittal, as an outcome. Nobody pretends that it leaves other birds alone and wishes them well, it doesn't. It's a bird that has adapted very well to the garden environment, and includes small birds and eggs among its summer diet. The evidence is incontrovertible. Only the wider implications can be open to question.

Have you ever been given a ticket for speeding? If you have, you will probably be

satisfied in your mind that you were unlucky to get it. Most of the time you are convinced that you drive as carefully as you can, generally within the speed limit. You are much better than many others. Now that you have been convicted you will have a criminal record, of course, but you are not a criminal.

Ground Force

If you were then told that the Magpie spends most of its time in laudable activities such as eating insects and removing corpses from roads, what would you say to that? Over the course of a year some seventy per cent of its foraging is ground-based, and on the ground it is unlikely to come across any offending balls of feathers that it might rip apart. Another percentage of time is spent higher up in trees, where it is still not threatening to its smaller neighbours. The destruction of junior birds, real though it is, is a fringe activity, undertaken for a very short period each season. For the rest of the year, Magpies are not in the business of attacking and killing adult birds, because for the most part the smaller birds are too quick for them to catch. The occasional murders do happen but they are rare, if unpleasant, events.

It should also be said that Magpies, if you could ever class them as 'criminals', are very poor ones. They almost always get caught, especially since they target nests and make the owners very distressed and noisy. If Magpies are raiding nests in your garden, the chances are you will either see them doing it or strongly suspect them of it. But for every Magpie raid, there are other, more subversive ones happening elsewhere. Cats are abundant, dangerous and clandestine killers. Squirrels, rats, weasels and Great Spotted Woodpeckers are all quieter, and lethal in their secrecy.

And what of the charge that Magpies reduce songbird numbers in the neighbourhood? Well, if you wish to be empirical about it: when a Magpie kills a brood of songbirds, of course it reduces their numbers. But aside from that, many other factors are always working in bird populations at the same time. If populations are declining, it is

The Magpie actually finds most of its food on the ground, and only rarely raids nests.

experience of Magpies, and allow the scientists free rein. It is extremely easy to see a Magpie take the nestling Blackbirds from our garden and extrapolate our observation to the whole country. Yes, a Magpie has killed birds in my garden – but does that mean it is happening everywhere else? Perhaps you have a stomach ache; perhaps several of your friends have a stomach ache. Does that mean that the whole of Britain's population has been similarly stricken?

There is also a danger in putting two and two together to make five. In recent years, there has been a sudden drop in the national population of Song Thrushes, and at the same time a rise in the number of Magpies in gardens. It is tempting to make the link, especially because we know that the latter sometimes prey on the former. However, the link is not necessarily valid. In recent years the number of people killed in road accidents in Britain has fallen, while the number of cars on the road has increased. Does that mean we should increase the number of cars to cut road deaths?

As it happens, the decline in Song Thrushes probably has rather little to do with Magpies. The main problem for the thrush seems to be adult mortality, not nestling or fledgling losses, which puts Magpies out of the picture completely. For the moment, in the light of reasonable evidence, no link between the Magpie and any other songbird population has been proven. The overall case against the Magpie, as decimator of bird populations, is distinctly tenuous.

Of course, if you hate Magpies, you'll not care about the scientific argument. That is your choice. If you see a Magpie raid and are upset by it, you are being gloriously and unashamedly emotional. Without our emotions we would not feed birds, and put up nest-boxes, and put money and effort into our wild neighbours' welfare. In the end, all this Magpie business really shows is actually something very uplifting - that we care.

usually for a variety of reasons. It could be increasing conurbation in the area, more pollution, a greater use of herbicides, or even a natural fall in numbers caused by bad weather conditions in previous months. It could be disease, too. Bird populations are very complex indeed, and always hard to understand.

A More Complex Picture

The garden, too, is in itself partly to blame. We all spend a lot of time saying how wonderful they are, but gardens themselves are seldom the top, prime habitat for birds. For example, when Blue Tits are breeding in healthy woodland they lay an average of about eleven eggs; in the garden, however, where food is much harder to come by, they tend to lay only six or seven. Another problem with gardens is their layout. Most are not substantially overgrown, and their hedges and borders are neatly trimmed. They make rather easy places in which to find nests, even for you and I, so it is not surprising that Magpies and other predators can do so too.

So, bearing in mind that bird numbers are delicate and impenetrable things to understand, what of the charge that Magpies have affected the bird population at large? This is the only charge that could be used to justify a cull.

What we must do at first is to cut out our own

The Chaffinch and Its Allies

THE LIVES OF some birds, superficially similar, can turn in completely different directions on the basis of a small pivot of behaviour. The same sort of divergence may happen to two people who are siblings: one small decision at an important point in life can turn one brother or sister into an unqualified success (e.g. avoiding drugs), whereas the other's fortunes could nosedive and leave them on the streets (e.g. taking drugs).

The Chaffinch and the Greenfinch are both finches, and both common garden birds, yet their lives are very different, especially in the breeding season. And the key to the difference is in their respective baby food. One feeds its nestlings entirely upon insects, while the other feeds its young largely (although not entirely) on seeds. This might seem to be a mere nugget of detail, but it has surprisingly wide ramifications for the birds' lives as a whole.

There's an important distinction between these two foodstuffs. Insects are everywhere. The Chaffinch, which is the insectivore of our two finch examples, can find plenty of food within a few metres of its nest. Any ordinary garden tree will play host to thousands of caterpillars, and the nearby air will be dense with flying insects. The Chaffinch can bring offerings of food in its bill to its young every few minutes.

Seeds, on the other hand, are less easy to come by. Seed-bearing plants grow in patches, which may be some way apart. No small area will hold enough seeds to feed a family of Greenfinches from hatching to fledging. So, to provision themselves Greenfinches must travel considerable distances around the neighbourhood. They make infrequent and irregular visits to the nest, feeding their young by regurgitation.

The most important implication of the Greenfinch's 'choice' to use seeds is that it completely rules out the possibility of defending a territory. A Greenfinch is only a small bird, and it could not possibly patrol an entire neighbourhood to keep other competing

With its long tail and slim body, the Chaffinch is well suited to catching flying insects in mid air.

Greenfinches away from its food-plants, however much it might exhaust itself trying. So Greenfinches don't bother to hold territories as such. Everyone forages over the same general area and shares the same seed supply, ruling out a great deal of competition. Metaphorically speaking, all the Greenfinches in the area buy from the same shops.

Neighbourhood Groups

Because Greenfinches have no need for a territory, except in the immediate vicinity of the nest itself, that means that they have no need to avoid each other. They can be sociable. Several pairs will often build their nests a few metres apart, sometimes in the same tree, and the birds involved will get to know each other so well that they will go out to hunt for food together, preen near to each other, look for water sources together, and generally work as an informal team. They will visit the garden feeders together and perch atop the Leylandii in groups, showing the world that they are part of a gang.

The Greenfinch eats many different kinds of seeds, including docks and sorrels. But seeds are always patchily distributed, and must be sought over a wide area.

Meanwhile, the Chaffinch, with an abundance of insect food, can and does defend an exclusive territory. Each pair lives a self-contained existence in the summer, and will take a dim view of any other Chaffinches using their territory as a food source. Breeding Chaffinches are not remotely sociable, and have no desire for teamwork. They require no help from others, and have no interest in giving it. They might visit the garden's food sources in the summer, but only as a pair and only occasionally.

The different way that Chaffinches and Greenfinches organise their social lives in summer also has a bearing on how they choose their partners in the first place, and carry on their lives as pairs. The male Chaffinch, knowing that he will need a territory for the spring, leaves his winter flock early and becomes a loner. He will find his own patch and sing a stereotyped, formal song to keep other males away. A listening female, on hearing his efforts, will make a direct approach and, if all goes well, the two birds will pair up quickly. The territory is now jointly owned, and will be the scene for all their pair-bonding and pair-affirming behaviour, including every step of courtship from initial interest to copulation.

Greenfinches, quite naturally, do things completely differently. Their winter flocks are an extension of their well-developed social lives, and most birds probably pair up within that flock, getting to know their partners over a prolonged period. The males don't sing stereotyped songs in their own specific sites, but impress the females by singing informal ramblings without much structure. They regularly launch into the air, treating their significant others to song-flights in which they describe wide circles and figures of eight at rooftop height. It's only when these females are sufficiently smitten, and the pair is officially formed, that they will find a nest-site and establish a small territory around it. By then much of their pair-bonding and sexual behaviour will already have happened, in 'public' places accessible to any other birds.

As a result of its summer diet of seeds, a male Greenfinch also has a little more work to do than a Chaffinch to help its mate while she is nest-building or incubating. To make good any shortfall in a female's diet, the male Greenfinch brings his mate food-parcels of seeds both before and during incubation. These will keep her going. The female Chaffinch, with such an abundance of food on her doorstep, needs no such help from the male. While incubating the eggs she takes frequent breaks, and finds all she needs during this off-duty period. There is little or no intimacy over food provision.

To look at them, you are almost bound to recognise that Chaffinches and Greenfinches are closely related, with their similar shape and similar behaviour in the winter. But because of their divergence over baby-food, they are as different in their breeding habits as a duck is from a sparrow. Well, almost.

Woodpeckers as Heroes and Villains

A VISIT BY a Great Spotted Woodpecker to a bird table or hanging feeder is always something of an event, especially in June when the red-capped youngsters may come along too. Woodpeckers are dramatic birds, bold black-and-white and red, and their entrance inevitably has a sense of drama about it. When the woodpeckers land, the smaller stuff often hangs back, or even

scatters, seemingly nervous of that mighty bill.

Earlier in spring that same long, chisel-like beak is put to other uses. From January onwards it is hammered very rapidly into a sonorous piece of wood to make a pleasing 'drumming' sound, the equivalent of a song. And it is also used throughout the year as a heavy tool for excavating holes. This is the woodpecker's great talent: it

Great Spotted
Woodpeckers are efficient
nest-predators and are
more than capable of
drilling through the wall
of a nestbox.

makes holes in the trees from scratch, making new homes where before there were none. It makes them for a nest cavity and for a roosting hideaway, adding new models again and again.

Excavators-in-Chief

The woodpecker often chooses to work on wood that is slightly rotten. It will hack away steadily, like a labourer might use a pickaxe. It is heavy work. After a week or two of intermittent effort the woodpecker will have made a substantial cavity, and so it starts working from the inside rather than the outside. By the end of the excavation the wood chips are gathered in the bill and tossed dismissively out of the new home.

It takes a very special bill to wreak this kind of destruction upon rotten, or sometimes even upon live, wood. That bill is also used for chipping wood-boring insects into view, or for ripping off bark, whatever it takes to provide a diet of arboreal invertebrates. A woodpecker would hardly be a wood pecker without it.

And, if you think about it, a wood would hardly be a wood without a woodpecker, either – at least, ornithologically speaking. Where, for example, would the tits breed, and the flycatchers? Many other birds besides woodpeckers rely on tree holes for their nesting sites, and the rest cannot excavate them for themselves. They depend on the woodpeckers to do it for them. If it were not for the activities of the carpenters of the bird world, all these species would be hard-pressed to find breeding sites at all.

In view of this, one might think that woodpeckers would be among the most welcome of all birds around the woodland or garden scene. And yet, when birds such as tits come across Great Spotted Woodpeckers in the breeding season, they repeatedly mob them aggressively. They fly towards the woodpecker, call loudly and try to drive the unwanted visitor away – perhaps away from a hole that, ironically, the source of their rage initially created itself.

One wouldn't expect a bird such as a tit to be clever enough to recognise the woodpecker and thank it politely for constructing its nest-site, but such a reaction does seem puzzling. Until, that is, you realise that the Great Spotted Woodpecker, despite its positive effect on bird populations, also has a dark side.

It's too easy, you see: a bill adapted for ramming through wood to find invertebrates can

very easily be put to a different investigative use. Should a woodpecker develop a taste for bird meat, it would have no trouble at all in finding some. In the average wood or garden there are plenty of occupied holes with nestlings in them in spring, just waiting there ready to be eaten, uniquely accessible to a hunter with a pickaxe. And this is exactly what happens.

A Great Spotted Woodpecker is an adaptable bird, and may be seen to hunt nestlings in several ways. The commonest technique is the logical progression from its usual feeding routine. It detects nestlings by ear as they call from their chamber at the bottom of the hole, and then it simply drills straight through to them. Within minutes the small bodies can be dragged through the newly created gap, one by one. In the second technique, a woodpecker lands close to the nest-hole and the nestlings, hearing the arrival of a bird outside, eagerly jump up to the entrance as they always do, hoping to be first to reach the expected parental food delivery. But they are met at the entrance by the woodpecker, and ironically become a food delivery themselves.

In many areas, including gardens, Great Spotted Woodpeckers have also quickly recognised that nest-boxes are also excellent and reliable sources of nestling meat. They are easier to get into than tree-holes, too, with thin sides and vulnerable entrance holes that can be quickly enlarged for forced entry. Predation by woodpeckers appears to have increased in Britain as more and more of these intelligent birds have cottoned on. Great Spotted Woodpeckers, you might say, are the new Magpies, with similar colour and similar tastes.

There are, however, more concrete solutions to this problem than offered by the Magpie controversy. Well, actually, not quite concrete, but 'woodcrete'. This tough substance, a mix of wood chippings and concrete, is the basic constituent of many new (and unfortunately pricey) nesting boxes, and provides a safe haven for younger chicks. An older method, that of placing a metal plate around the nest entrance, was effective for deterring the woodpeckers from forcing their way in from the entrance, but never prevented their more determined operations to drill through the side. Now, perhaps, nest-boxes made of less penetrable material will eventually cause the box-raiding habit to decline.

And if it does, Great Spotted Woodpeckers will be raised to home-grown hero status again, at least in the garden environment.

Leave it Alone!

IF YOU WERE walking along a street near your home and happened to spot an envelope containing a thousand pounds in cash, you would probably find yourself in a dilemma. What to do: should you pick it up, pocket it and consider yourself its new owner, or should you take it to the police and let them try to contact the previous one? Your resulting course of action says a lot about who you are.

Whatever your decision, though, it is unlikely that you would have ignored the envelope. That would have handed the dilemma to the next person who came along, and who knows if they could be trusted? There is something about a thousand pounds in cash that precipitates at least some form of action.

Tiny Mites

Every summer, in every neighbourhood in Britain, people are faced with a similar problem. But it's not a wad of cash that they find, but a tiny, open mouthed, often cutely fluffy baby bird.

Let's face it: it's almost impossible to be dispassionate about these tiny mites. They look helpless, incongruous and abandoned. Their very disposition cries out for intervention, for making things better and, yes – for some kind of decision. But what to do?

There are two types of these babies. There are the wretched and naked ones, with the outsize heads and mouths, the ones that lie prostrate on the ground and could easily be stepped upon. Such nestlings have no chance. Only about one in ten eggs survives to become a breeding adult, and this poor wretch is in its column with eight others. If you find one, leave it alone with a clear conscience.

The second type of baby is the appealing, well feathered one, the sort that hops about and cheeps and apparently implores you to pick it up. Please don't. Intervening with such a chick could actually cause it genuine harm. As long as you are in physical contact with it, the parent bird, which is inevitably nearby, cannot feed it and is in a state of severe stress. In such situations you are not ameliorating the problem, you are the problem. If you think in its position it is vulnerable to cats then, fine, take it to a safer spot

a short distance away; the parent won't abandon it because you've touched it. But otherwise leave it alone – and take your cat indoors. If it really is abandoned it will succumb anyway, and you are left with your conscience clear.

Cute and vulnerable, a baby bird like this young Song Thrush cries out for intervention – but resist the temptation!

If you do find a fluffy chick on the ground, and you know that the nest is nearby, on no account try to put it back. When small birds are about to leave the nest they have a special escape response when faced with danger: they all abandon ship and explode from the nest prematurely, landing out of immediate harm's way but facing an uncertain future. If you try to put an itinerant chick back with its siblings you run the risk of causing a mass break out, to the detriment of all the hapless birds involved. Not only will your chick be back on the ground, it will now be joined by several others, all endangered by what you have done.

So, please, remember this season's mantra and spread it to all your friends. If you find a young bird, it's not your responsibility – leave it alone!

IF BIRDS said goodbyes, June and July would be full of them. For many of the species in the garden, these are the months when the young birds become independent. Once parents and young split, that's it; they do not socialise or have regard for one another in the future. If anything, the two generations could become rivals.

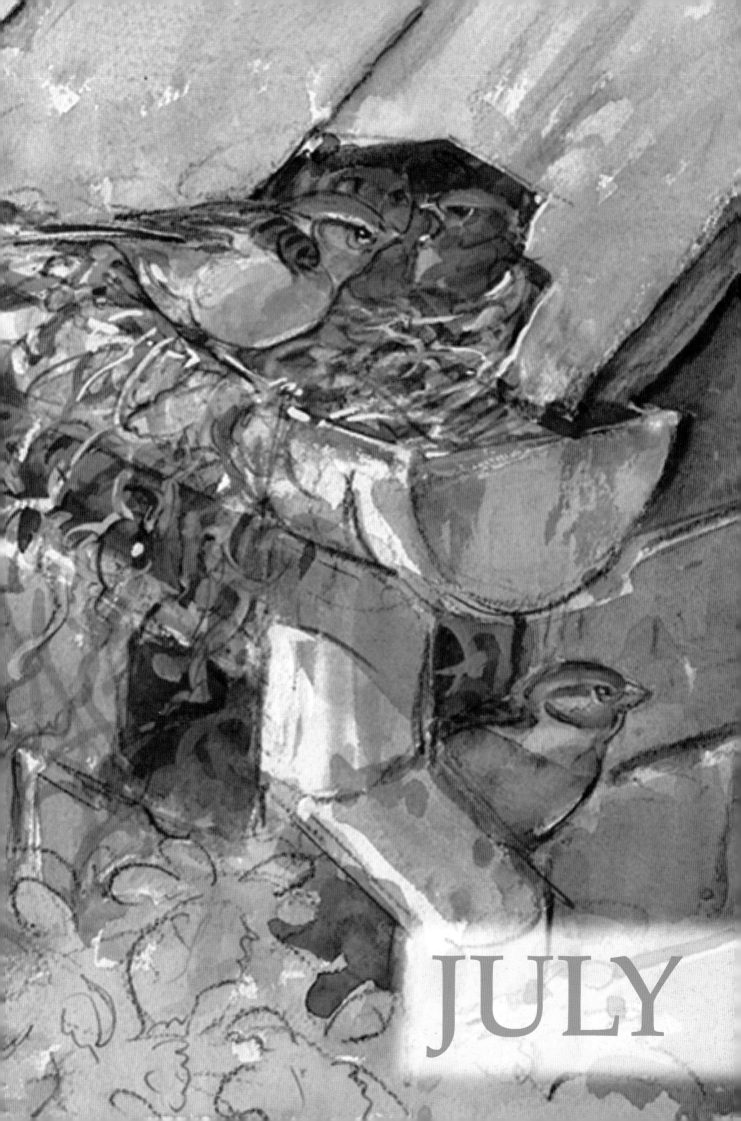

JULY

Fledging

When a young bird leaves the nest, it becomes a fledgling, not a nestling, and in its limited way it is already a success story. Not all eggs hatch and not all nest-bound young survive, so it has started life beating the percentages.

But the next few weeks will be exceedingly perilous. Many predators lie in wait for it, taking advantage of its poor co-ordination and limited flying skills. Hunger also threatens: a newly promoted fledgling leaves its cosy existence without many fat reserves. The weather, with all its unpredictable moods, is set to frustrate it, too, making the basics of its life potentially very difficult. But at least it has one advantage. Its parents, having devoted so much effort in bringing it up to this stage are not ready to abandon it just yet.

The nest that was once the young bird's dwelling place is now fully consigned to its past. Most young birds, having fledged, never return to their nest, not even at night. A young Great Spotted Woodpecker, for example, spends its first night as a fledgling out in the open, and so does a Blackbird, Blue Tit or Robin. There is no such thing as a home comfort for a young bird. It is simply too dangerous to return.

Fledglings rarely have the look of being at one with the world. They inevitably seem forlorn and frayed at the edges. Their bodies have put so much effort into growing quickly that their feathers have come off second best, giving them a fluffy, unfinished appearance, with short wings and tail. Most retain a hint of the gape that served them so well in the rough and tumble of the nest, thus betraying their babyhood, as if nappies were showing through their teenage clothes. They perch with a precarious hold, and fly without taking account of obstacles. They crash into things and get into trouble, like youngsters everywhere.

They might look delightful to us, but one of these incompetent balls of feathers is utterly

defenceless, and thus an easy meal for a predator. Sparrowhawks pick them off in such numbers that they can support clutches of their own hungry young. Magpies and Carrion Crows, too, which for much of the year do not bother with live bird food, also tap into this supply of ready meals. And cats patrol gardens, mopping up fledglings without requiring much stealth or cunning.

Once they have left the nest, the fledglings wander away from their erstwhile nurturing place, never moving much further than the edge of the neighbourhood, but nonetheless keeping on the move throughout the course of a long July day. The siblings of the party often spread out slightly, remaining within hearing, but necessarily visual range of the rest of the family. Should one youngster be grabbed by a cat or Magpie, this spacing ensures that the others are not sitting ducks for a return visit – or at least, not ducks sitting side by side.

Tutorials

Broadly, though, the family keeps together, so that the parents can keep feeding each fledgling without wasting too much energy. Foraging sessions can also become tutorials, valuable lessons for the future. It will not be long before the fledglings are independent, and it is essential that they pick up some of the tricks of the trade to

Previous Page: A House Sparrow brood about to leave the nest.

Right: Fledglings like these Great Tits tend to look a little frayed at the edges. In the nest, most energy is put into growing quickly, not into producing immaculate plumage.

When faced with danger, a young fledgling's only hope is to freeze and fall silent like this Spotted Flycatcher, hoping to be overlooked.

cope with the shock of isolation. So a Green Woodpecker on a lawn, for example, can make a hole in the soil and lap up its favourite ants in front of its watching student young. A Great Spotted Woodpecker might escort its progeny to a hanging nut feeder. Greenfinches may perch side by side on sunflowers with their fledglings, cracking open seeds. And Song Thrushes might even run snail shell-smashing seminars with their attending brood.

For some species, the learning curve to attain proficiency is exceptionally high. The fledglings effectively become long-term apprentices to their parents. Young Sparrowhawks, for example, stay under the parental tutorial wing for a whole month after fledging, often throughout July. Presumably they watch the adults at work and improve their own hunting techniques day by day as they do so. Their departure from total dependence is a gradual process, yet also a very natural one. The apprenticeship ensures that the young catch enough food to wean themselves, step-by-step, off their parents' offerings.

Youthful Tawny Owls, too, take a very long time to cope with the demands of nocturnal hunting. The young leave the nest looking fluffy and flustered, about as dangerous to the world at large as a child's soft toy. Having fledged in June, in July they will still be sitting helplessly on high perches, beseeching their parents to fill their empty stomachs. By August they will have started hunting, and by about September they will surprise their providers one gentle night by finally giving up on their easy food. Their apprenticeship has lasted three months or more, a lengthy introduction to self-sufficiency.

Of course, most small birds have much less time than this. Young tits, led into a canopy of leaves almost dripping with caterpillars, are feeding for themselves after only a week. Starlings are independent of their parents within days of fledging and form flocks with their peers. But these are unusual. Wrens, Robins and Dunnocks along with most other small birds, take up to two and a half weeks to become totally self-sufficient.

One might be tempted to ask why parents do not lavish even more time on their progeny. After all, if the average small bird clearly requires a week or so of post-fledging care, why stop then?

The benefits of parental protection are obvious. Would not an extra helping of tutelage make the next generation's entry into a hostile world even more assured?

Of course it would. But in a society where everyone is short-lived, there comes a point at which parental care is a luxury, not a necessity. Remember the breeding maxim: productivity is everything. The year has been a success - great! The young have left the nest and are approaching independence. Now productivity takes a longer term view, towards another breeding attempt next year. A selfishness surfaces in the inner bird. With the footsteps of the young going out of the door, the parent bird's emphasis shifts towards self-preservation, towards keeping in good condition, and towards ridding itself of the burdens and dangers of excessive parental care. The young must go!

Of course, for a great many garden birds, the instinct to boot the fledglings out into the wider world as soon as possible has a much more urgent significance. The summer has not yet passed, food is still plentiful, the adults have made it through parenthood unscathed, and they just about have the energy to do it all again. They are to be second brooders. All their days of agony in early spring really have paid off, for they are to be doubly productive. For these supreme achievers the young are an impediment; they might even be forcibly driven away. They are fit enough to take their chances, and that's that.

Splitting the Brood

Quite a number of bird species, among them Blackbirds, Song Thrushes and Robins, have

Within days of leaving the nest, young Starlings are completely independent.

allowing just the one run at breeding, but with a potentially high yield. The tits go for it, like gamblers in a game of high stakes.

Blackbirds are not gamblers, and they are not reliant on a single productive event. They feed their early broods on worms, and add helpings of caterpillars for their second set of offspring. Their second clutches, laid at the height of summer, often contain more eggs than the first ones, since food is more plentiful at this time for the resulting chicks. But over the course of the season Blackbirds spread out their productivity, making breeding less dicey, but gaining lower rewards. If these birds were human they would invest in blue-chip companies.

New Recruits

Several other species, including Carrion Crows, Magpies, Great Spotted Woodpeckers and Tawny Owls, breed just once a year for the simple reason that they cannot fit a second attempt in; their breeding cycle is simply too long. By and large these are longer-lived birds than tits or Blackbirds, and have less need to make an impact in a single breeding season.

And so, by the end of July, many breeding matters have been settled. The lawns and borders of the garden are home to a veritable army of independent birds, many of them new recruits which, freed from dependence on their parents are now no longer called fledglings, but juveniles. They will never formally cross paths again with their hard-pressed guardians, who invested such efforts in them. Indeed, many of those same hard-worked adults are into their second spurt of production. Already high producers among the population, they are doubling their productivity, and their progeny will have the benefit of good genetic material. Success, quite literally, breeds success.

There is one final section of bird society for which the month of July could bring a late bloom. These are the birds that failed to find a mate at the start of the year but, by virtue of their species being double-brooded, now have another chance. Divorces do happen, and mates do change. Mishaps kill off healthy parents, and others become exhausted. Every population of birds contains a "floating" element and for a few fortunate ones, July is the beginning of an Indian Summer.

found something of a happy medium. Each of them may be double, or even triple-brooded, yet they are reluctant to let their responsibilities towards the latest young slip completely. When the fledglings of these birds leave the nest, they are looked after by both parents at first, but then each youngster is informally assigned one adult to take sole charge of it, a practice known as 'brood-splitting'. With a reduced workload, the female can begin to feed up, build a nest and form the next clutch of eggs inside her.

In other species, there is simply a shift in responsibilities towards the male, who sees the fledglings through their steps towards independence on his own while the female is away on renewed breeding duty. As the youngsters grow, so his duties begin to subside, and he can begin to sing again.

In gardens, there is quite a sharp division between species that have only one brood, and those that try to rear several. Blackbirds, for example, rarely settle for only one nesting attempt, whereas Blue Tits, Kestrels and Carrion Crows rarely or never try twice. The differences reflect their contrasting lifestyles.

Blue, Great and Coal Tits are birds that literally lay all their eggs in one basket. Their breeding season is short, acutely timed, and explosively productive, with their outsize clutches of ten or more relying completely on the glut of caterpillars that appear on the leaves in early summer. At this time of year a single large oak tree may be home to 100,000 larvae, ten times as many as the birds will need. It's a reliable bloom, predictable but short,

The Woodpigeon's Bonanza

IF BIRDS WERE cars, the Woodpigeon would be one of those heavy models, like a Cadillac, that uses up a lot of gas. With a big tummy and an appetite to match, the Woodpigeon rumbles through the neighbourhood as a symbol of good and easy living.

Appearances don't deceive. Few birds have a more straightforward time than this portly pigeon, especially in the period between July and early October, the harvest time in the arable fields of Britain. The Woodpigeon can obtain its food requirements very quickly at this time of year, spending a mere five to ten per cent of the day feeding. It only bothers to forage in the early morning and late evening, and the rest of the time is devoted to loafing, preening and sex. It sounds like the ideal summer.

The month of July marks the start of the Woodpigeon's main breeding season. This, of course, is far later than for most birds, but it is highly convenient for a bird that feeds mostly on grain. With wheat and barley ripening in the fields to yield vast supplies of food, the Woodpigeon's eyes must go moist with delight at the prospect of such easy reproduction. All a pair has to do is to build a reasonably secure nest, and the rest should go swimmingly.

The birds don't even make much of an effort. Their nest is a pile of carelessly interwoven sticks placed unimaginatively in a tree fork or in the branches of a bush. It doesn't take long to build and, frankly, it looks like the cheap model it is. The birds lay only two eggs, and these are coloured an unexciting, economy white. The

incubation period is short and sweet – just seventeen days.

All pigeons have a big advantage over other birds when it comes to feeding their young. Instead of bringing in insects or seeds as the environment provides them, pigeons refine food within their digestive system and make a special concoction for the chicks. It is a curd-like substance formed by the crop, and it's called pigeon 'milk'. It's full of protein, fat and certain vitamins, and it gives the young pigeons, known as squabs, the perfect start in life. They grow faster than other young birds, and are soon prospering well ahead of species of comparable size. Only two other types of birds, penguins and flamingos, feed their young on 'milk', so the young pigeon is from unusual stock indeed.

With their big appetite for hard, dry grain, it's not surprising that Woodpigeons are also enthusiastic drinkers, and visit water sources several times a day. Even in July there are usually plenty of sites around, especially in gardens. But if water is scarce these birds are strong and powerful fliers and can commute

Sitting pretty: the Woodpigeon's fine plumage is rarely appreciated, reflecting its abundance and perhaps our ambivalent attitude towards success.

considerable distances to reliable sources if necessary. They quite frequently alight on the water surface in their exuberance to quench their thirst, and are perfectly capable of swimming.

Another unusual adaptation to make a pigeon's life easier is its ability to suck water straight into its mouth and down its throat. The vast majority of bird species cannot do this; instead they take a scoop, tilt their heads right up and let gravity do the work for them. So why is the pigeon different? It's easy to jump to the conclusion that its method is more efficient: a pigeon should be quicker than

Pigeons are among the few birds that can actually suck up water, rather than scooping it up and lifting their head to let gravity do the work.

another bird in obtaining what it needs, thereby decreasing the time it is vulnerable to predators. But surprisingly, tests have shown the two methods of drinking to be equally efficient, so that's not the answer. Instead, it would appear that pigeons are better able to make use of very small, temporary water sources than other birds, such as shallow puddles made by a rain shower, or gatherings of droplets of leaves. It makes sense. If you needed to drink from the surface of a leaf,

what would you use: a teaspoon or a straw?

With these special talents at its disposal, and with a diet that is easy to obtain, the Woodpigeon, not surprisingly, is a highly successful species, and recently it has topped at least one count as Britain's most numerous bird. Unfortunately this success has led to conflict with those people who work the land. The Woodpigeon's love of grain has made farmers see red, and the knives have been out in an effort to control its numbers. Many methods have been used, including shooting, scaring and poisoning. Whatever its level of success, this war on Woodpigeons has certainly made the arable fields of Britain, legendary for their supposed tranquillity, into something of a battlefield.

Success Story

The problem is that we and the Woodpigeons enjoy the same food. Conflict between pigeon and man is inevitable. Look at this list of items that attract feeding Woodpigeons, and compare it to the vegetable matter than can be found upon your kitchen table: wheat, rye, maize, sugar beet, turnips, cabbage, Brussels sprouts, oats, cauliflower, lettuce, mustard, radish and peas. Does the list make you feel hungry? If you were a Woodpigeon it would whet your appetite as well.

It's hard to believe, but a few years ago the Woodpigeon population in Britain was actually declining. But, in line with this bird's usual good fortune, a new crop was introduced that was especially to its liking, and the population did an about-turn and rocketed back upwards. The crop was oil-seed rape. At the same time there was a general switch towards autumn sowing on farms, and that was another boost, too. This species, it seems, can do no wrong.

It's good to report a success story. With so many birds living lives on a perpetual knife-edge, it's satisfying to know that some have an easy lot instead. Whereas a Blue Tit is a pauper living in a crowded tenement, the Woodpigeon lives in a large villa and puts its feet up. Don't blame it! Next time you buy a lottery ticket, ask it to coo the numbers for you.

Having a Bath

ON A HOT July day it is hard to resist the sight of water. For most of the year the bird bath is usually the least exciting – albeit vital – part of our wild bird husbandry, a necessary provision that is used quite fleetingly and provides much less interest than the feeding stations. But today the birds are queuing up to use the facilities, waiting their turn like ladies at a theatre loo during the interval. The water source is the hub of the garden's entertainment.

The bird visitors alight near the precious resource and hop into the centre of the shallow pool. Cautiously and watchfully, like bathers on a beach changing behind a towel, they squat a little, ruffle their feathers, put their head and breast down and flutter their wings, so that drops of water spray all over their plumage. They might do this several times, with interruptions to check for danger, but their sessions are invariably short. Bathing is fun and

A Swallow dip-bathing. Very occasionally the manoeuvre goes badly wrong; there are records of pikes in a pond grabbing dip-bathing birds in their waiting jaws.

important, but, being out in the open, is extremely perilous.

The aerial birds have a more exotic method of bathing. Swifts, Swallows and House Martins simply fly down towards the surface of a pond or stream and skim low over it, so close that, at one point their belly actually touches the water. They don't land at all, but instead, with a flick of the wings, carry on upwards and away, their bellies dripping and leaving an invisible vapour trail.

When a bird bathes, it normally only moistens its plumage slightly, leaving it bedraggled but not saturated. The main function of a quick dip is simply to allow the feathers to be preened more easily. But from time to time a bird will have a good soak, too. This extra immersion serves to clean the feathers and the skin underneath. A good bathe on a hot day is also great for cooling off, as one might expect.

Dust Bathing

Bathing in dust is less easy to explain. It's a common sight, though, especially among groups of House Sparrows. Finding a safe place on the ground, often on the edge of a flower-bed, the sparrows squat on the earth or dust, and follow much the same routines as they would for more normal bathing, ruffling their plumage and flicking the dust particles all over their bodies. They clearly revel in their immersion and, once they have finished, give themselves a tremendous shake, much as we might dust ourselves down after lying on a sandy beach. The precise reason for dust-bathing is not certain, but it probably serves to remove stale preen-oil and other detritus from the plumage.

Sometimes it rains on a July day, filling up puddles and dispersing the birds to many different bathing points. But why wait for pools to form? Why not make for a high perch and have a shower instead? This is what the Woodpigeon often does, and it makes a comical sight. Perched atop a roof or chimney pot the bird holds on tight and lifts one of its wings, as if it were about to squirt deodorant under its arm. It doesn't quite hold position there, though, but raises the wing higher still so that it is almost over the bird's back. This obviously enables water to trickle to those parts that other forms of bathing cannot reach. It's so satisfying that, after a short time, the bird switches sides and lifts its other wing in the same curious, over-balanced posture, and then embarks upon some blissfully contented, post-shower cooing.

For sheer usefulness, however, there is no form of 'bathing' better than lying in the sun. It might seem strange to us that birds should practise something that we consider such indulgent relaxation, but this is no luxury: sun is very important for a bird's well-being. For a start, a spot of sunning can help to get a bird started in the morning, warming it after a chilly night. But there is more to sunbathing than this, because birds actively seek exposure to the sun during the hottest part of the day, too, when there is no need to tweak the metabolism.

Sun Comfort

The benefits of sunning are wholesale. It helps, for example, to get the main flight feathers back into shape after they have been bent around by wear and tear. The sun is good for a bird's skin, too, and when mixed with preen-oil on the rump, it synthesises vitamin D. The heat from the sun might make that same preen-oil run more freely over the feathers, assisting in its distribution plumage-wide. And it might make a bird's usual feather parasites more active, causing them to go walkabout and become easier to remove.

All of these various forms of bathing, from basking in the sun's rays to letting rain fall all over the body, come under the umbrella term of 'comfort behaviour'. Although birds indulge in them all throughout the year, they are rarely more obvious than on a hot summer's day, and dust-bathing, for one, is certainly stimulated by high temperatures. On days when we might feel lethargic and in need of invigoration, it's interesting to know that the birds out there in our gardens are feeling exactly the same.

A sunning bird like this young Blackbird squats down, ruffles its plumage and spreads its wings and tail, remaining motionless except for rhythmic panting.

Birds and Mud

IT MIGHT NOT always seem like it, but heavy rain in the breeding season can be a good thing. So long as the shower doesn't last too long most birds can ride it out with little difficulty. And a good downpour also has a particularly useful by-product: mud.

A surprising number of garden birds use mud as a nesting material. Blackbirds and Mistle Thrushes put it around the inner edge of their cup nests, with just a thin lining of grass separating the eggs from the hard material. Song Thrushes actually lay their eggs directly upon a hard plaster-type substance made up of mud, dung and rotten wood. Carrion Crows, too, place soil within their nest structure. For these species mud

is one ingredient among many, useful for part of the structure and integral to it, but they only need to make a few trips to a puddle or to the side of a garden pond in order to gather enough.

To the Nuthatch, though, mud is far more important, and it uses substantial amounts collected over a long period. Nuthatches are hole-nesters with lots of competitors, especially Starlings. When building the nest the female Nuthatch plasters mud all over the entrance hole, to fit her exactly. The hole is then too small to allow a Starling in. If there is plenty of rain in the spring the Nuthatch can complete the job before the Starlings attempt a take-over. If progress is too slow the Starlings are able to make headway in

House Martins need plenty of mud for their nests, so they suffer if the spring weather is too dry.

House Martins make rare visits to the ground when collecting mud for their nests.

demolishing the Nuthatch's handiwork. There is a kind of race here, one bird adding mud, the other removing it, and the Nuthatch can only win if mud is abundant.

Mud Cons

But no birds rely quite so much on good mud supplies for their nests as the House Martin and the Swallow. For these species, mud is the primary component of their structures. The House Martin builds a cup under the eaves of a house, with an entrance hole just below the roof. It sticks a few feathers in, but essentially the nest is made entirely of mud pellets, between seven hundred and fifteen hundred in all. Both sexes build the nest, and it can take ten days to complete. House Martins breed in colonies, and on a big nest-building day dozens of these two-toned birds, with their white snowshoe-like feet, will descend to puddles to collect their material. It is one of the few occasions when these aerial birds can be seen on the ground.

The Swallow builds a similar type of nest to that of the House Martin, but places it upon a horizontal surface. Among the pellets of mud the Swallow sticks in various organic materials, including twigs, grass and horsehair. These sundry additions are important, because they make the nest structure more malleable, and less likely to fall apart if the mud shrinks or expands when it gets dry or wet respectively. Swallows

also pay attention to the type of mud that they use: if there is too much sand, the resulting nest will be liable to disintegrate during the time that young are in the nest. But if they use too much clay, it will be more difficult to build in the first place. Both Swallows and House Martins use the thixotropic quality of mud – the fact that it becomes easier to mould when stirred by the bill – to enable them to build the nest and judge whether they have the correct sort of mixture.

Needless to say, all these birds suffer when mud becomes scarce, particularly in drought years. If your garden has a pond, they should be fine. But it might be worth hosing down a patch of earth in the flowerbed for them every so often. Certain of your garden birds will be very grateful indeed if you do that.

Britain's Most Dysfunctional Bird?

CONSIDER THE CASE of Britain's most dysfunctional bird. The case is purely for interest, and we can make no judgements or draw any conclusions. It merely offers the chance to put the magnifying glass upon an individual example and see how far away birds can stray from our expectations of 'normal' family life.

The bird is a Cuckoo. Already everyone knows that the females lay eggs in the nests of other species, and fob them off to foster parents for their entire childhood. So immediately our Cuckoo is a candidate for the social workers. But

what makes this particular Cuckoo a little unusual is its origin. As an egg it was not laid by the female you might expect, the one that spent the spring defending its own egg-territory from other females. It was laid by an interloper, an opportunistic female that wandered in the breeding season from territory to territory, and came upon this particular patch of ground by chance. The visitor laid its egg surreptitiously when the owner-female was occupied elsewhere. So not only was this egg laid by a Cuckoo – a species described as a brood-parasite – but actually it was laid by a parasite upon a parasite, an unwelcome guest in the territory of another unwelcome guest.

Complicated Upbringing

As for the father, that could have been anyone. Female Cuckoos often mate with several males, and who knows which one of them was the father of our case study Cuckoo? In any case, our bird will never meet either of its parents, and even if it did, it would not recognise them, at least as far as we know.

How about the foster parents? Did our Cuckoo strike lucky with these? Were the parents a monogamous item, a chance to right the wrongs of a splintered and abandoned childhood?

Probably not, if they were Dunnocks. These small birds practise a very rare mating system in which individuals regularly have multiple partners. Both sexes may have multiple partners at the same time, in fact. So if you were looking for a stable home as we humans understand it, having a 'pair' of Dunnocks as foster-parents would not be the answer. Although you would know who your foster-mother was, a succession of two or three males visiting to feed you would not help to establish your identity very clearly.

By the time it had left the nest, our case study Cuckoo would be opening its mouth wide, making loud begging calls, and attracting a succession of smaller birds to its cause. Besides Dunnocks, any number of other small, insectivorous species might be called to its pleadings, so inviting and hard to resist is its open bill. It would recognise its foster-parents as they came, perhaps, but as to the rest: who on earth are they?

So here's to our dysfunctional Cuckoo. Every concept of parenting that we understand is eschewed by its species, right from the genetics to the duty of care. Its blood parents were not in a stable relationship, and gave it up for adoption at birth. It was a displaced egg, laid in a borrowed nest in a borrowed territory. Its foster parents were of a different species entirely, and although their relationship was stable, there were other birds involved, too, to further complicate its upbringing. When a little older, and a fledgling, it was fed by its foster parents, but with help from several unfamiliar faces and unfamiliar species that it had never seen.

That, you will agree, is the profile of a very confused young bird. And sadly, the signs are not good. Rumour has it that it was already a mass murderer before it left the nest, and was suspected of killing all of its foster siblings. And the trouble it will cause has only just started.

Brought up in care – a fostered Cuckoo will never meet its true parents, so far as we know.

AUGUST IN the garden can have the feel of a stadium after a football match. The game has been played and the cheers of the crowd have subsided, leaving a sensation of emptiness where before there was energy and vibrancy. Even the bird feeders, the scene of such passionate battles in late winter and such earnest visits in spring, are for once strangely empty of customers.

AUGUST

Days of Ease and Leisure – and Preparation

PEOPLE OFTEN MENTION that their favourite bird, usually a Robin, seems to disappear in August. The garden spade rests curiously unadorned and the bowls of mealworms remain untouched; they wonder if, at this late stage of the summer, the bird has somehow succumbed to illness or misfortune. But it is not generally so. August is the month of a bird's annual moult, a time for retreating into the depths of bushes. The Robin goes undercover as it swaps its old feathers for new ones.

Changing feathers is one of those tasks that besets birds each year, and that they probably face with the same minor dread that might afflict us over a visit to the dentist, or an annual appraisal at work. The moult is inevitable and necessary, but it takes away much of a bird's energy and verve. It could be compared to adolescence in humans, where so many of the body's resources are diverted to growth that a little grumpy listlessness is inevitable. The moult also renders birds unusually vulnerable to the run-of-the-mill threats that constantly loom over their everyday lives, the hunters such as cats and raptors. So it's not a time for exuberance.

Feathers are remarkable structures, made of the protein keratin. They are highly complex at a microscopic level, with branches branching from other branches and interlocking with tiny hooks to make them what they are: light, but strong and resilient. The birds of course work them to death: flying, landing, taking off and occasionally knocking themselves on perches or obstacles. And feathers aren't everlasting. They wear out after a while, just as our clothes wear out if we don them frequently enough. The birds moult while we pay a visit to the high street shops.

If a bird were to change all its feathers at once – not advisable – it would become temporarily bald and flightless, and as edible and accommodating as a pre-packed chicken. So the moult is staggered over a month or so, with feathers being replaced slowly. The large feathers of the wing are changed in sequence so that a bird's flight is not fatally impaired on any particular day. The long procedure must be an inconvenience and a bore, but it is essential that it should be this way, for sheer survival.

Making Statements

Besides being simply a system of replacing worn out feathers, the annual moult can also be used to make statements. Many garden birds, such as Chaffinches,

Previous Page: *Adult and young Goldfinches on thistle seeds. The young lack patterning on the head.*

Left: *Ragged Robin – during their annual moult many birds hide away in thick vegetation.*

Greenfinches, Pied Wagtails and House Sparrows moult into dowdy versions of their spring or summer selves in August, mainly to become less conspicuous, but also partly to preserve the impact that the breeding plumage will make when it is acquired next year. Their plumage is saying, one might suppose: 'I'm not interested in breeding just yet', and all around will get the message.

The moult can also make more positive and challenging statements. Up until now young Robins that have fledged in June or July have retained the plumage of their youthfulness: spotty and brown, with a hint of peacekeeping ochre on the breast. But in August, they moult away their retiring personality and become closely similar in appearance to the adults, equipped with the full blown red-orange breast that acts as a permanent territorial challenge to other birds. The change means: 'Treat me like an adult, now. I'm a threat to you like anyone else'. The red is the badge of maturity, and the young of the year will no longer be treated with indulgence.

Many juvenile birds put on the uniform of adulthood or near-adulthood in July or August. Blackbirds lose their spots and turn out black or plain brown, tits exchange their yellow cheeks for white cheeks, Woodpigeons touch their necks up with white patches, and young Great Spotted Woodpeckers slip off their crowns of red. Some might leave hints that they are still very young – male Blackbirds have a black, not yellow bill, for example – but generally these former fledglings have cast off the fluffiness and aerodynamic awkwardness of a month or two back. They have come far, and have the feathers to prove it.

In the weeks following their eviction from the parents' territory, many youngsters exhibit a distinct tendency to wander, a phenomenon rather grandly known as post-juvenile dispersal. This is another reason why the garden can appear to be so dead in August; all the young have left and gone elsewhere. Most remain within a few kilometres of their birthplace, but some move considerable distances away, sometimes to a different region. It's thought that they spend this peripatetic time assessing the qualities of whichever local area they find themselves in, noting potential places where, in the future, they might hold a territory and breed. Nobody is quite sure of the deeper reason why this travelling is necessary, but it might help them to avoid the territory of their parents, or to ensure that siblings keep well apart and prevent the possibility of inbreeding.

Birds caught by this urge to disperse soon find others doing the same thing, and join forces. One of the delights of August birdwatching is to watch these roaming flocks of juveniles travelling together around an area, checking it out like a crowd of shoppers at a car boot sale. The surprise is that not one, but several species of birds may take part together, moving along in one large, somewhat informal party. Blue Tits will travel with Great Tits, and both will be joined by Treecreepers, Goldcrests and warblers such as

August sees Blackcaps busily feeding up prior to their southward migration.

Blackcaps. If your garden backs on to several others, or you adjoin an area of woodland or scrub, you are bound to be visited by one of these mixed flocks once in a while, which will pass through over the course of ten minutes or more. You never know quite what will be in the party. Many a garden watcher has seen an unexpected Nuthatch or Lesser Spotted Woodpecker gracing their garden in August, never to return.

Although August is a summer month, it has, especially by the end, the distinct whiff of autumn about it. The days are shortening, and everyone in the wild knows it. The resident birds cast half an eye on getting ready to face the winter to come, and those birds that travelled here to breed, the summer visitors, will soon be in migratory mode again. August is a month for preparation, for whatever obstacles lie ahead.

And it's a good time for provisioning. The days are still satisfactorily long to give the birds plenty of time to fill their stomachs, a myriad of insects still crawl around the trees and bushes or zip through the heavy air, and both the tended

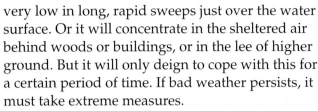

very low in long, rapid sweeps just over the water surface. Or it will concentrate in the sheltered air behind woods or buildings, or in the lee of higher ground. But it will only deign to cope with this for a certain period of time. If bad weather persists, it must take extreme measures.

In fact, Swifts can tell very quickly if bad weather is approaching, for there may be a perceptible drop in the numbers of food items wafting around the atmosphere, even when the depression is still five hundred kilometres (300 miles) away. With this early warning system in place many birds, especially those that are not breeding, have the choice to opt for avoidance, rather than riding out the inclement conditions to come. Despite being attached to the colony, they leave the area temporarily, not staying around to be rained upon and to be blown about. The Swifts, one might say, take flight.

And so the retreating birds begin a journey. Despite the fact that it could be midsummer, and that they are not due to migrate for many weeks, they nonetheless embark on a round-trip that

Once they leave the nest, these young Swifts may not touch solid ground again for two years.

could take them several hundred kilometres away from their breeding, or potential breeding colonies. If they were human they would get in a car and just keep on driving until the skies were clear. As it is they fly into the wind, in a clockwise direction, skirting the front and taking a short-cut south or south-west to the fairer weather behind. Their remarkable storm-avoiding movements quite regularly take them to the Continent and back, and the whole trip may be as much as two thousand kilometres (1250 miles). And for the duration of their trip, these restless Swifts are, at

least technically, British birds.

The Swift's remarkable ability to avoid weather fronts is made possible by its celebrated aerodynamic shape. With their streamlined bodies, tiny feet and long, sickle-shaped wings, Swifts are expert gliders, moving great distances without many wing-beats, saving energy like the albatrosses of the Southern Oceans. Swifts are also, as their name implies, extremely fast through the air, and can travel several hundred kilometres a day effortlessly. These attributes have conferred on the Swift by far the most aerial existence of any living bird.

High Flyers

Although breeding Swifts sleep in their nests, non-breeding birds are famous for their ability to cat-nap on the wing, and to stay aloft throughout the short summer nights. On the warmest evenings of the year, it's possible to watch them as they first fly over in screaming, circling parties, then rise higher and higher into the air as darkness gradually falls, eventually being lost to sight. They will rise to a height or between a thousand and two thousand metres (3250-6500 ft), or occasionally higher, and maintain their lift by flying into the wind and alternating flaps and glides. Here they undoubtedly doze and lose some of their alertness, although it seems unlikely that they sink into the depths of sleep. By dawn they are on the way down again, circling until they once again reach the aerial plankton layer. Here they will stay for the rest of the day, where, unfettered by breeding activities, they can spend their time feeding and watching the world from their elevated viewpoint.

It has been said that a young Swift, not breeding until it is nearly two years old, has no cause to touch down on something solid, from the point that it takes its own first flight to the point that it first lands near its own first nest site some twenty months later. Although that is hard to prove, there is little doubt that some non-breeding Swifts simply spend the entire season flying around the vicinity of their usual or prospective colony. These birds do not land at all. By day they fly low, by night they fly high.

So, as if the short length of their stay were not galling enough, many of our Swifts don't actually set foot in this country even when they do come to visit us. If they really were dinner guests, we wouldn't invite them back.

The Thistle-birds

IT'S AUGUST AND it's part of bird lore that you shouldn't lay any eggs. That would be asking for trouble. With autumn lying in wait just around the corner, and with many insect populations rapidly on the wane, a prudent bird should really be concentrating on other things. Only the super-fit or the insanely optimistic would be foolhardy enough to go for a breeding attempt so late in the season.

But there is one garden bird that does often nest this month and whose nestlings routinely breathe autumn air – the Goldfinch. And this is for a special reason. For as soon as its young are a few days old the Goldfinch feeds them on thistle seeds. And thistles, of course, are one of August's bumper crops.

If ever a bird were associated with a plant, it would be this gorgeous creature with its equally colourful, if unloved, floral benefactor. Even the Goldfinch's scientific name, *carduelis*, means 'of the thistle'. In the wild, and in untended patches in gardens, you see them most often in small flocks sprinkled over the seeding heads. They search especially for the half-ripe, milky seeds that are easy to swallow, clinging on adeptly to an overhanging flower head and digging their bills in between the bracts to extract the seeds. Of our common breeding finches, the Goldfinch has the narrowest and longest bill, specially adapted for squeezing into confined spaces. With its small size, strong legs and light weight, it is also the finch most at home on the heads of standing herbs. It can cope with whatever acrobatics are necessary to keep feeding: it is as efficient hanging upside down as it is perched normally, and it can face upwards or downwards, whatever the need dictates.

Neighbourhood Groups

Goldfinches are rarely seen alone. In the summer they live in well-organised social groups consisting of a number of locally breeding pairs. The constituent pairs often nest close together, for example in the same tree or shrub, and work for much of the season as a team. Each day they forage as a flock, using all available pairs of eyes to spot the seeding plants, which tend to be patchily distributed. When their young leave the nest they remain in their 'neighbourhood group' until the advance of winter, when many migrate out of the country, and others join much larger flocks to roam the countryside.

It's easy to spot a recently fledged Goldfinch, especially alongside an adult, for although its wings are strongly patterned, it lacks the spectacular head pattern of black, white and red that makes a mature bird so distinctive. Instead, it has a streaky brown head, so pale as to show off its beady eye. It can look like a completely different species, and many are the garden birdwatchers who have phoned their local club to bring news of an exciting new August find. Even so, the company that these anaemically coloured birds keep should make their identity obvious, for in the early days their parents rarely leave their side.

Although the various species of thistle are undoubtedly important to Goldfinches - the seeds can constitute forty per cent or more of their annual diet – they visit a wide variety of other related species, including knapweeds, burdocks, dandelions, groundsel, ragwort and chicory. Another of their favourites is the completely unrelated teasel, a member of the scabious family. Various types of teasel can be bought from garden

The young Goldfinch, with its plain-coloured head, looks very different to the parent. It is best identified by the company it keeps.

The Green Woodpecker has a big territory and visits many lawns in the course of a day.

winged males and females of normal garden ants take to the air in what is known as a mating swarm. On just those few warm days ant fever grips the bird community. Swifts and House Martins are out in force, showing off their aerial expertise. Starlings, too, their triangular wings spread, show off an unexpected ease in the insect-rich atmosphere, flying high above rooftops. Flocks of Black-headed Gulls, just back from their coastal breeding sites, wheel over inland villages and snap up much smaller food than they are used to. Even House Sparrows, not normally birds to fly higher than they absolutely must, launch into the air, make a quick bill snap and drop down back to their elevated perches. And meanwhile, down on the ground, Robins and Chaffinches field the emerging lovelorn insects before they even have a chance to use their specially grown wings.

The sense of excitement around a mating swarm of ants is something special to behold in the garden. But it isn't the strangest association between bird and ant. That distinction goes to a very rare form of behaviour known rather unimaginatively as 'anting'. It's the sort of clandestine enterprise seen far more often in gardens, where birds can be intimately observed, than in the wild. Blackbirds and Starlings do it, and so do members of the crow family, such as Jays. If you ever see it, though, consider yourself extremely privileged.

Ant 'Therapy'

There are actually two different kinds of anting behaviour. In the form known as active anting, a bird will take some ants in its bill and wipe them all over its plumage, often taking some time to do it thoroughly, rather as a person might enjoy a massage or manicure. This is the version performed by the Starling and, unless you can watch the bird closely, it is very easy to miss. Passive anting is much more exciting. In this version the bird actually sits upon an ant hill or colony, and winds the workers up by shaking itself around a little and upsetting the nest. The furious colony members dutifully swarm all over its ruffled feathers, squirting out formic acid and generally acting aggressively. It's easy enough to detect a bird passively anting, for it will squat on the ground, spread its wings and tail, open its bill in ecstasy, and shuffle its feathers at regular intervals. To all appearances, the Jays or Blackbirds that do this enjoy it enormously.

It isn't difficult to guess why the birds might use ants in these ways. When the insects squirt out their acids and other secretions, the liquids go all over the plumage. The ants' attack is not feeble, like some demonstration with a water-pistol: the liquids are strong and noxious, and highly effective in defence. They are akin to a detergent, and are excellent for killing off all those irritating ticks, mites and insect parasites that are always found in a bird's plumage. Ironically, the anting bird is using insects as insecticides.

One question that one might ask is, if it's such fun and evidently effective, why doesn't every bird ant? And why don't the practitioners of anting do it more often? The answers to these questions are still a mystery, one more secret in the lives of our backyard birds.

The Thistle-birds

IT'S AUGUST AND it's part of bird lore that you shouldn't lay any eggs. That would be asking for trouble. With autumn lying in wait just around the corner, and with many insect populations rapidly on the wane, a prudent bird should really be concentrating on other things. Only the super-fit or the insanely optimistic would be foolhardy enough to go for a breeding attempt so late in the season.

But there is one garden bird that does often nest this month and whose nestlings routinely breathe autumn air – the Goldfinch. And this is for a special reason. For as soon as its young are a few days old the Goldfinch feeds them on thistle seeds. And thistles, of course, are one of August's bumper crops.

If ever a bird were associated with a plant, it would be this gorgeous creature with its equally colourful, if unloved, floral benefactor. Even the Goldfinch's scientific name, *carduelis*, means 'of the thistle'. In the wild, and in untended patches in gardens, you see them most often in small flocks sprinkled over the seeding heads. They search especially for the half-ripe, milky seeds that are easy to swallow, clinging on adeptly to an overhanging flower head and digging their bills in between the bracts to extract the seeds. Of our common breeding finches, the Goldfinch has the narrowest and longest bill, specially adapted for squeezing into confined spaces. With its small size, strong legs and light weight, it is also the finch most at home on the heads of standing herbs. It can cope with whatever acrobatics are necessary to keep feeding: it is as efficient hanging upside down as it is perched normally, and it can face upwards or downwards, whatever the need dictates.

Neighbourhood Groups

Goldfinches are rarely seen alone. In the summer they live in well-organised social groups consisting of a number of locally breeding pairs. The constituent pairs often nest close together, for example in the same tree or shrub, and work for much of the season as a team. Each day they forage as a flock, using all available pairs of eyes to spot the seeding plants, which tend to be patchily distributed. When their young leave the nest they remain in their 'neighbourhood group' until the advance of winter, when many migrate out of the country, and others join much larger flocks to roam the countryside.

It's easy to spot a recently fledged Goldfinch, especially alongside an adult, for although its wings are strongly patterned, it lacks the spectacular head pattern of black, white and red that makes a mature bird so distinctive. Instead, it has a streaky brown head, so pale as to show off its beady eye. It can look like a completely different species, and many are the garden birdwatchers who have phoned their local club to bring news of an exciting new August find. Even so, the company that these anaemically coloured birds keep should make their identity obvious, for in the early days their parents rarely leave their side.

Although the various species of thistle are undoubtedly important to Goldfinches - the seeds can constitute forty per cent or more of their annual diet – they visit a wide variety of other related species, including knapweeds, burdocks, dandelions, groundsel, ragwort and chicory. Another of their favourites is the completely unrelated teasel, a member of the scabious family. Various types of teasel can be bought from garden

The young Goldfinch, with its plain-coloured head, looks very different to the parent. It is best identified by the company it keeps.

centres, and these consistently attract Goldfinches, even when none are thought to be in the area. When the teasel's seed-heads are finally exhausted, they can be refilled manually with tiny seeds such as nyjer to keep the Goldfinches in stock.

Teasel is a tough plant with long spines protecting its seeds, and for Goldfinches its peculiar attributes literally separate the men from the women. Male Goldfinches have slightly longer bills than females and can reach the seeds of teasel directly, whereas females have to bend back the spines with physical force to probe their way in – hard work that they are reluctant to tackle. As a result, roaming flocks of Goldfinches using teasel are mostly males. This sexual segregation would at first seem to be a little unfair, effectively depriving females of an important food source, but with the males concentrating on teasels the females are at liberty to utilise thistles instead, a much more abundant and easily reached harvest.

In recent years Goldfinches have become an increasingly familiar sight in gardens. The trend towards summer feeding, and the availability of suitable food such as nyjer and black sunflower seeds has allowed Goldfinches to make use of hanging feeders with perches, as well as encouraging them still further to feed from lavender, teasel and cultivated varieties of thistle. The future for these specialised finches is looking bright, even though they will sometimes break one of the garden's golden rules, and nest when the summer is past its best.

Flying Ants and Ground Ants

ANTS MAY BE small, but they loom surprisingly large in the lives of several garden birds. Now in high summer, with hot weather around, these tiny insects are everywhere and ant-related incidents abound. It's a time for watching the birds very carefully, for there is a good chance that you might spot some unusual behaviour.

Many gardens, especially the larger ones, are likely to play host to the ultimate ant connoisseur. The Green Woodpecker may be a large bird, but its engine is fuelled by small bodies. In summer it eats almost nothing else but ants, and even

specialises on the smaller species; only in winter is it likely to make bold incursions up into the trees to take other types of insects. The Green Woodpecker will eat over twenty different sorts of ants, from the black ones or yellow ones on your lawn to the aggressive red ones that spoil your picnics. When it fancies a change in diet it simply switches to a different species – of ant of course.

It feeds mainly on the ground, but it's a shy bird and easily disturbed. If given the opportunity it will stay on your lawn for hours,

Black-headed Gulls wheel around the sky, feasting on flying ants.

doing battle with its soil-based prey. Often a Green Woodpecker will make a hole in the turf, right through the heart of a nest, and lap the unfortunate creatures up as they wander, one by one, along passageways suddenly exposed to the light. This arch ant-eater has a very long tongue that will stick out 6 cm (2.5 in) beyond its bill, and the tip of that tongue has a life of its own, reaching into holes and pathways, disturbing workers in every corner of their underground city. To make matters worse the tongue is thick with saliva, enabling it to slobber like a soppy dog and soak up all the ants. A Green Woodpecker attacking an ant colony must generate a scene that would do a disaster movie proud: bodies littered everywhere, wholesale destruction, mayhem among the survivors.

A few times each summer, in July or August, the Green Woodpecker's enthusiasm for ants becomes a more widespread obsession. It's a little bit like Wimbledon week, when a mainly indifferent British public suddenly becomes mad on tennis, and the sport has its moment of glory. This sudden excitement reveals itself when the

The Green Woodpecker has a big territory and visits many lawns in the course of a day.

winged males and females of normal garden ants take to the air in what is known as a mating swarm. On just those few warm days ant fever grips the bird community. Swifts and House Martins are out in force, showing off their aerial expertise. Starlings, too, their triangular wings spread, show off an unexpected ease in the insect-rich atmosphere, flying high above rooftops. Flocks of Black-headed Gulls, just back from their coastal breeding sites, wheel over inland villages and snap up much smaller food than they are used to. Even House Sparrows, not normally birds to fly higher than they absolutely must, launch into the air, make a quick bill snap and drop down back to their elevated perches. And meanwhile, down on the ground, Robins and Chaffinches field the emerging lovelorn insects before they even have a chance to use their specially grown wings.

The sense of excitement around a mating swarm of ants is something special to behold in the garden. But it isn't the strangest association between bird and ant. That distinction goes to a very rare form of behaviour known rather unimaginatively as 'anting'. It's the sort of clandestine enterprise seen far more often in gardens, where birds can be intimately observed, than in the wild. Blackbirds and Starlings do it, and so do members of the crow family, such as Jays. If you ever see it, though, consider yourself extremely privileged.

Ant 'Therapy'

There are actually two different kinds of anting behaviour. In the form known as active anting, a bird will take some ants in its bill and wipe them all over its plumage, often taking some time to do it thoroughly, rather as a person might enjoy a massage or manicure. This is the version performed by the Starling and, unless you can watch the bird closely, it is very easy to miss. Passive anting is much more exciting. In this version the bird actually sits upon an ant hill or colony, and winds the workers up by shaking itself around a little and upsetting the nest. The furious colony members dutifully swarm all over its ruffled feathers, squirting out formic acid and generally acting aggressively. It's easy enough to detect a bird passively anting, for it will squat on the ground, spread its wings and tail, open its bill in ecstasy, and shuffle its feathers at regular intervals. To all appearances, the Jays or Blackbirds that do this enjoy it enormously.

It isn't difficult to guess why the birds might use ants in these ways. When the insects squirt out their acids and other secretions, the liquids go all over the plumage. The ants' attack is not feeble, like some demonstration with a water-pistol: the liquids are strong and noxious, and highly effective in defence. They are akin to a detergent, and are excellent for killing off all those irritating ticks, mites and insect parasites that are always found in a bird's plumage. Ironically, the anting bird is using insects as insecticides.

One question that one might ask is, if it's such fun and evidently effective, why doesn't every bird ant? And why don't the practitioners of anting do it more often? The answers to these questions are still a mystery, one more secret in the lives of our backyard birds.

House Sparrows Have Holidays

HOUSE SPARROWS ARE real stay-at-homes. Once they have ceased their early wanderings as juveniles looking for a home, or males looking for a territory in spring, they remain faithful to an area and their chosen colony for the rest of their lives. If you have House Sparrows in your garden, therefore, you can view them as neighbours, or as familiar local characters that you might love or hate. The oldest recorded sparrow lived for over twelve years, and it's certain that it never travelled more than a few hundred metres away for all of that time.

Except, that is, in August. For during this month all the members of the colonies that live in rural or suburban areas suddenly leave their precious territories, and go on an annual pilgrimage that could be viewed, with a little imagination, as a holiday. For a week or two your garden will be empty of these overbearing chatterboxes, and it might seem eerily quiet.

They have not moved far – none travels more than about two kilometres (just over a mile) in all – but they don't return at night. They are going where all the other sparrows are going, to the farmland where the seeds in the fields are ripening. It will be a great sociable binge, with all the sparrows mixing together to exploit a brief time of plenty. It's crowded, often overwrought, and for a short while territories and borders are completely forgotten.

If sparrows ever let their hair down, August is the time. Next month they will return, well fed and refreshed, and settle down to their sedentary lives once more.

People go to the seaside, sparrows to farms. Both are places of crowds, hot tempers, sociability and heavy eating.

THE BREEDING season just past has been like an explosion. Way back in spring the fuse of reproduction was lit. The 'bomb' went off and dozens of small birds burst first from the nest and then from their parents' territory. In August this feathered debris sailed around the neighbourhood and now at last, in September, some at least has floated to the ground and has settled in a new place.

SEPTEMBER

Moving In, Moving On

AUGUST MIGHT BE a month to yawn and doze, but September ushers in the autumn with a little more urgency. The wild fruit is still heavy and succulent upon the berry-bearing trees, and there are still bees and flies aplenty visiting the dahlias, chrysanthemums and Michaelmas daisies. But the occasional sharper night whisks away the heavier air. Mornings are often misty, and dampness begins to pervade the soil. September has a gentle but persuasive way of introducing harder times.

It's the official first month of autumn and the many of the local young birds have come to choose the garden as their new haunt, with a view to becoming a permanent resident. Meanwhile the adult breeding birds wake up from their moulting slumber and re-inhabit the patch they so vigorously defended up until a few weeks ago. Most species don't lay much formal claim to it, since they will not need to declare it

Mornings are often the best for garden birdwatching, especially after a chilly night when the weak rays of autumn sun are especially welcome to a foraging bird. The Blackbirds are soon bickering over the stocks of berries on the hawthorn, rowan or pyracantha, chasing other birds away from their bounty with the fervour of an over-zealous security guard. In between skirmishes they move to gobble up the orchard fruits, which are freshly covered in dew and shine with the same unreal lustre that one sees on apples and pears in TV commercials. Starlings, harried from the berries, fly down to the lawn and strut across it in gangs, poking into the tired grass for invertebrate helpings. Blue Tits forage among the rose beds, not so much after the hips but after the aphids on the underside of their leaves. They use their acrobatic gifts, so evident when hanging from bird feeders, to get to any

Above: Once a young Nuthatch has settled into a territory in its first autumn, it will remain within it for life.

Previous page: Swallows gather on wires prior to their migration.

again until the spring. But Robins and Wrens are exceptions. Their territorial boundaries are heatedly and sometimes violently reinforced from now onwards, throughout the autumn and winter and right up until the patter of tiny feet breaks the barriers down again for a short period next summer.

leaf, no matter how awkwardly placed. And Greenfinches make brief visits to the lawn, probing for the fallen seeds of grass, or for the powder-puff heads of dandelions. For these resident birds it is business as usual, hunting for food intently, but without much real urgency.

Hungry Migrants

But on some September mornings different kinds of feeding birds mix with the residents. Perhaps a bright yellow Willow Warbler will pay the garden a special visit as it flits amongst the leaves of a shrub, or a Blackcap will hide in the hedge, only showing itself when it reaches for a particularly awkwardly placed berry. These birds are transients, and they bring the reality and miracle of migration right to our own back door. They will have arrived overnight, probably starting their journey between eighty and 150 kilometres (50-100 miles) further north, and they will be acting very hungry. Although they have built up some fat reserves for their journey, that process is not yet complete, and they cannot waste the days when resources are still available fresh from the foliage. Much leaner times and meaner places lie ahead.

Look up and you can also watch migration happening above you. The chances are that, if you train your eyes for long enough on any September morning, you will see Swallows and House Martins streaming over, wherever in the country you live. They will probably be high up, not much more than dots, and you can tell they are on the move by the determined way that they are flying. House Martins usually drift around and sail in little arcs, but not today; they have ground to cover and have set their sights high.

There is a frisson of excitement to be felt when you see migrant birds over your house and in your garden, knowing that these very travellers are headed for distant, exotic lands. You imagine their destination and get excited for them by proxy. It's like the thrill you get when you board a train that takes you to the next town, yet has a final destination much farther away, in some different part of the country or even a different continent. During your short stage it is easy to contemplate just sitting there and staying on, imagining what it must be like to go to the track's farthest reaches, where life is a bit different.

Migratory Adventures

Many people dread for the future for bird migrants, and especially for 'their' Swallows or martins, the ones that enliven the days of spring and summer for their admiring households. They have seen documentary footage of balls of feathers dead in the Sahara Desert, of birds shot in the Mediterranean, or those blown into the sea by cruel winds. They imagine that migration is so dangerous as to be some exotic form of suicide. But it isn't. Migration is a risk, true, but every year millions of birds survive it quite easily. They might have their adventures along the way, but these are often no more life threatening than the hazards they might face any day here. Most migrants can cope with these readily enough; they are built that way. And the British winter, for many a small insectivorous bird, is a much more deadly prospect than a month or two of flying to the sunshine.

Even so, our migratory birds do undertake an extraordinary feat. One marvel among many marvels is that every bird, with a few exceptions, takes on its journey alone, with not a jot of help from anyone else – not its parents, nor its siblings, nor any benevolent old-timer it might meet along the way. It leaves of its own accord, navigates with brand-new, untested orientation equipment, enters completely unknown lands and continents without a map, and even knows when it has arrived at its destination. It does, of course, encounter other birds of the same species along

The autumn garden is still heavy with fruit – more than enough to satisfy this Blackbird.

the way, and may feed alongside them in a Saharan oasis, for example. It might even form temporary flocks with its peers. But these flocks are informal, no more a support system than might be found among a loose aggregation of human hippies following the Silk Road, friends one day, yesterday's acquaintances the next. The journey, and the destination, is the bird's to make and the bird's to guess, all alone.

Much has been learned about bird migration over the years, but nothing has yet been able to demystify it. The more we know, the more we wonder at the phenomenon. For example, the certainty that a particular bird will actually set off and not remain stubbornly on its breeding grounds seems to be controlled by the chemical changes in an internal year-round clock, the make-up of which is still largely a mystery. At the end of its trip something internal also tells a bird that it has arrived, but again, we don't know for sure what. But about the journey, and the orientation systems a bird might use – we know plenty about them.

Consider, for example, a bird's use of the stars. There is no dispute that some species can orientate using the celestial sky; captive birds put into planetariums can be seen to follow constellations when these are shifted artificially.

But how they originally learnt to do this, we'll never know - and can only speculate. Experiments have shown that juveniles are not born with a map of the stars in their brain, but have to learn their patterns and movements by themselves. On an autumn night, just imagine this as you lie in your bed: at the same time as you are resting, a young bird, barely out of the egg, is looking up on a clear night and observing how the stars rotate around the northern pole.

Obviously, birds using the night sky have to migrate nocturnally, and shift from their usual daytime routine. They rest and nap in the late afternoon, and then, as the sun begins to set, prepare for departure. They set off about half an hour after sunset, then fly for a few hours before landing in the dead of night at a completely unknown place. There they will sleep and wait for the dawn. Only when a migrant has been on the move for several weeks will it get used to its nocturnal shift patterns, and fly for most of the night.

If this new unknown place is your garden, feel privileged; your land is a stage in a great journey. For a day or two your visitor will treat you as a motorway service station, with board and lodgings attached. It will feed and rest, preparing itself to move on.

Far from the garden – birds on the move, setting out on their long journey across the sea.

Trapped by bird line – this Redstart is just one of millions of migrating birds that never make it past the Mediterranean.

Fantastic Skills

The majority of small birds migrate nocturnally. This allows them to use the daylight hours to refuel. And darkness confers other benefits, too. Air currents have usually calmed down in the lower atmosphere by nightfall, reducing any problems with wind. The cool night air prevents the bird from overheating, a considerable advantage bearing in mind the amount of energy it is using. Hazards will be fewer at night, especially the flying ones that might catch you; they are at roost. So small birds, flying at perhaps 300 m (1000 ft) above ground, have the skies to themselves, and the best of the conditions.

Another benefit of night flights is that, when the birds actually depart, at dusk, the position of the sun is still obvious, and can be used for orientation. This type of direction finding is easy – we could do it too. With the point of the setting sun to their right, we and they can simply go south until its effect disappears.

Some birds do, however, migrate by day. Swallows and martins are in this group. They are able to refuel on flying insects as they go, a bit like marathon runners taking sips of water along the way, but not stopping. But how do they navigate? It seems certain that they orientate themselves by means of the sun, as a night migrant will do as it sets out. But they don't use its sunset or sunrise point. Instead they can follow the sun's position in the sky, using it for directional modifications as it appears to move from east to west in the course of a day. What is astonishing about this is not the observation of such an obvious celestial body, but the birds' ability to calibrate its movements with their own internal body clock. The sun is no more than a very rough guide to direction finding unless you know the time, but birds do. Somewhere inside them, an accurate time-keeper ticks away.

The majority of birds also use another fantastic skill to help them, their sensitivity to the Earth's magnetic field. This is a gift we don't have, of course, and can barely imagine. Birds do not orient themselves away from magnetic north, as if they were using a compass, but can detect something much more subtle. The Earth is like a large magnet, and lines of magnetic field run from the south pole to the north. It's these field lines,

and their angle of inclination back towards the north pole from the fat area around the equator, that the birds can detect and use to position themselves. If you find this concept hard to grasp, don't be surprised; it is quite abstract to us, and beyond our experience. The birds don't understand it either, but they use it effortlessly.

Besides the sun, magnetic field and stars, birds use other clues, too. On their return journey in particular, many use landmarks to pinpoint their home areas, features such as rivers or forests or coastlines. Their internal aptitudes seem to know no bounds. Scientists have discovered in various birds the ability to detect polarised light, infrasound (very low-pitched sounds, inaudible to us), wind currents, directional scents and barometric pressure, all of which may or can be used to help birds find their way. The truth is, most birds use lots of direction-finding parameters, switching from one to another with ease. A small bird is equivalent to a high-grade computer in its ability to travel with great accuracy, like a living micro-chip, programmed for migrating vast distances.

September sees the peak of migration away from this country. By its end, most of our summer visitors have fled. However marvellous their journeys are, we can feel flat when they are gone. In a sense they are taking our fair weather with them, too, and their loss heralds the strengthening of autumn. From now on, all thoughts are on the grim reality of shorter days, and the long battle for survival ahead.

Strife among Robins – the Fat Lady Sings

OF ALL THE birds in the garden, none is more territorial or aggressive than the Robin. It might look attractive and friendly to us, but that pleasing colour on the breast is a permanent warning to other Robins not to intrude upon its boundaries at any time. Every adult Robin effectively wears an unchangeable T-shirt carrying the slogan 'Buzz Off!'

For the last few weeks these highly strung birds have languished in the thick bushes of the garden and kept an unusually low profile. The months of July and August are the time of their annual moult, when Robins must save their energies to grow new feathers. It was a time for a territorial cease-fire. But now, in September, with a flash new cut of orange upon their fronts, these fierce birds are ready to show off their true colours again, in every sense.

Months of strife lie ahead. Back in the spring, when the last serious battles raged, it was adult versus adult, male against male, fighting for territories in which to bring up their young. They were tough days, but the issues were simple enough. Now things are very different: not only are the newly fledged kids ready on their blocks and gunning for a fight, but so too are large numbers of adult females.

Go out into almost any garden in September, and you'll hear Robins singing, almost ceaselessly all day long. It's a good time to impress friends with your bird song knowledge, since almost every other bird is quiet, and you can declare 'Oh, that's a Robin' with refreshing certainty. These singers are a little less tuneful than the Robins in spring; their song has a more melancholy, appropriately autumnal air. And the voices are mixed. The males are singing, as usual, but they are joined by females, too.

This is extremely unusual. Female birds of any kind only occasionally sing, and it is almost unknown for them to use this form of communication to defend their own territory, especially one that is not shared. But Robins are a significant exception. These combatants are females entering into a world that is predominantly male, like women who take up boxing, or drive heavy goods vehicles. It's a rare form of sex non-discrimination.

The stakes in autumn are different from those of a few months before. The Robins are still fighting over land, as previously, but now it is for a different reason; they are trying to acquire and defend feeding territories, not breeding territories. Every individual, male or female, needs its own private patch to feed effectively.

When you think about it, it makes sense. The Robin feeds mainly by patient observation, watching for movement on the ground below while it is perched up at a convenient height, on a low branch for example. It is waiting for an insect to come out of its hiding place in the vegetation and wander across the lawn or the leaf-litter. Having spotted a movement, the Robin flits down and grabs its meal, despatching it with relish. But imagine what would happen if it had to share its feeding sites with another bird. They could find each other jumping down to the same meal, or disturbing one that the other has been waiting for. It would be annoying and distracting.

Red-breasted Hotheads

A territory-holding Robin, then, is a real hothead. It gets livid when disturbed by another Robin, and when any other birds come past and interrupt its foraging. Dunnocks, which live in similar places, are frequent victims of the Robin's ire, and there are records of it attacking most other common garden birds. It will even attempt to drive away small mammals, such as field mice, if they are in the wrong place at the wrong time.

Scraps with other birds are short-lived, and blow out quickly. But competition between Robins is deadly serious, and has far-reaching consequences for survival. In September, at the time of re-establishing territorial boundaries, a bird's future prospects can hang in the balance. This is why Robins can become not just unpleasant to each other, but violent too.

Trouble starts when one bird ignores the formal rules of land ownership, and trespasses into another's territory, effectively ignoring the song of the incumbent. It may be seeking an extension of its own territory, or be trying to usurp the whole package. Song is a statement of ownership that carries some weight; most birds accept a singer as an owner, and are submissive if they should intrude into a territory. But troublemakers brazenly enter the disputed ground, accompanied by the tune of their rival. The moment they do so, tension grips the air.

The birds first trade insults. Each sings directly at the other, throwing phrases out alternately. This is not normal, laid-back song, but a different, strangled kind, with such fast delivery that the birds appear to be falling over their words in anger. Thus engaged in their quarrel, the birds might continue in this public shouting match for half an hour or more, sometimes exchanging songs for angry 'tick' calls, and regular flicks of the wings.

If after some time tempers have not cooled, the threatening noises become accompanied by threatening postures. As people, we might start shaking our fists, or making gestures with our fingers. Robins draw attention to their red-orange breasts instead. They fluff out their front feathers and stand tall and strong, like an opera singer about to belt out an aria. If their opponent hops above them, they will throw their head back. Should they be on a higher perch, they will lean over, with their tails in the air. Whatever they do, the message is clear. The red means: 'Get out, now, while you have the chance'.

By now, any intruder will have shown itself to be very bold or very foolish not to have fled. In the vast majority of encounters, song or postures will have done the trick. But occasionally, with diplomacy

and shadow-boxing exhausted as options, there is no alternative but to fight.

Robin fights are not pretty, and if you like Robins you won't want to think about such things. They are rare, too, settling perhaps less than one per cent of disputes. They are also very quick – shockingly quick, in fact, if one ball of feathers never gets up again. There are no rules of engagement, just violence and blood.

They begin without a bell, when one bird goes for the other – a quick strike with foot or bill intended to knock the challenger to the ground. If this is successful there will be a rapid struggle, with each bird kicking and pecking. The birds may rear up, breast to breast, flying against each other, or they may roll over and over on the ground interlocked. This is mid-fight, and if a bird is losing, it's a last chance to escape injury or death. A few more struggles, and the stronger bird begins to win. Pinning its antagonist to the ground, it kicks and pecks at the eyes and skull of the other bird. The vanquished bird is injured. Bleeding and in pain, if it can it will wrestle free; this is its last chance. Otherwise it will succumb to its fate, and never dispute another territory again.

Song, threat and physical combat, then, are the Robin's tools for keeping out the neighbours. Song keeps rivals at bay, though they might still occupy adjacent territories; threat displays are perhaps more intimidating, and usher the intruder well away. Fights settle matters completely. A dead Robin can't argue back. And then the fat lady sings.

Robin fights are quick, shockingly violent, and rare.

117

The Swallow's Long Journey

WE IN BRITAIN can be a bit parochial. We think of Swallows returning in spring as our own personal property, coming back to their rightful home. We watch them swoop and swish over fields of long grass, dodging black-and-white cows and touching the tops of poppy-bleeding fields, and consider them quintessentially English. One Swallow does not make a summer, we sigh, referring to their lengthy stay here for the best of our weather and our longest days.

But there is another country for which one Swallow would not make a summer, either, and it's in a different hemisphere: South Africa. For the people of that part of the world, the coming of Swallows in November and December is as much a sign of summer as the same bird's emergence in the northern hemisphere. It seems that this well-travelled bird is welcomed almost everywhere it goes in the world.

In recent years a great deal has been discovered about the more mysterious part of a Swallow's life, the journey in between its breeding grounds here and its wintering grounds there. And now, owing to the tireless work of those who put rings on thousands of birds' legs and hope for the occasional recovery in some far flung spot along a bird's way, we have a few tempting clues about the actual route that our Swallows take, especially in autumn. We don't have the complete picture yet, but we know enough now to cheer them almost every step of the way.

The Swallows remain around their breeding sites late into the summer until, at the end of August, they finally depart for the year; they will be back in March or April. Their first migratory journeys will be in short hops of a few miles, to places where it is safe to roost at night. These are the days and weeks when we see so many Swallows on wires, twittering to each other and restlessly shifting about. They make progress slowly, gradually going south, until the barrier of the English Channel faces them, usually at some time during September or October. At this point some Swallows have an advantage: a brief hop across only thirty kilometres (20 miles) of water. Others further west have a longer haul. But wherever they step over, the Swallows now move south over a band of coastal France about a hundred kilometres (60 miles) wide. It's been

several weeks since they set out, and they are beginning to make faster and faster progress, buoyed by good fat reserves and a steady start.

When the Swallows reach the Pyrenees they do a curious thing. Instead of flying over the mountains, they head east along the northern rim, until they see the Mediterranean for the first time in the very north-eastern part of Spain. Some strike out straight over the water, passing over a considerable barrier of sea before calling in on the Balearic Islands to refuel. Others drop down the coast of Spain.

Into Africa

Either way, the Swallow's journey now takes it to North Africa, and the looming Sahara Desert.

The birds have instinctively been expecting a major barrier. They are designed and prepared for it and, during this outgoing journey at least, the Saharan section seems to be completed, surprisingly, without much bother. Now supremely fit from their journeys, the Swallows overfly the desert usually in one long haul. Although a few travel along the fringe of the desert, near the west coast of North Africa, most appear to go straight across it.

The next stage where Swallows have been recorded is in West Africa, in Nigeria. Here many British Swallows encounter a hazard of gigantic proportions, a human tradition of slaughter at one of their major stopping off and roosting points. At a place called Ebok Boje, over a hundred thousand Swallows are killed annually for human consumption, captured at night at their roost in the elephant-grass. It is a place of great peril for Swallows from all parts of Europe. And, who knows, perhaps there are other places like this with similar slaughter among the less well known parts of the route?

The Swallow's trail now goes cold for a few thousand kilometres, and – if if you like – it disappears out of radio contact. From Nigeria it moves east and south into the giant forest belt of Central Africa, to places so remote that, of all the people we meet or the animals we see, perhaps only the Swallows have ever been there. They must zoom over the tops of the monster forest trees, gleaning tropical insects that humankind

Almost there – British Swallows in transit through Africa.

has never seen or described. Or maybe they jump from open space to open space, brushing past lions and elephants. Whichever way they go, the Swallows are now coasting, managing many kilometres a day as their destination nears.

Preparing to Stop

It will be only a few weeks before the great forests eventually give way to more open country, and the vast distance of Africa begins at last to run out. The Swallows press on, not relieving the pace, but inside their bodies their chemistry is preparing to stop them. No one knows how, but somehow the Swallows now cease their journey in just the right place so that, so far as is known, few if any fly out beyond the Cape and into the oblivion of the Southern Ocean.

And so, by December, Christmas time for us, the Swallows have swapped their hemispheres and returned to their favourite season, the summer. They settle in Botswana, Namibia, or South Africa, have a moult, and cross paths with other Swallows from all over Europe and western Russia. In less than two months they will be on their way back again.

The Swallow's long journey, occupying the four months from September to December, is quite a leisurely affair. But soon, with their stomachs full of African insects, the birds must go back, and the return trip will be a different matter. In travelling to South Africa the birds were concerned mainly with survival, and completing the marathon to their wintering grounds. But on their way back north, the birds will be in a hurry, participants in a race.

There is no place for a slow Swallow. The fastest birds will win the best territories, and also the aces in the pack of cards required for breeding. Remarkably, a fit and experienced Swallow can make the journey from South Africa to Britain in the space of five weeks, travelling about three hundred kilometres (190 miles) a day.

Perhaps at that rate the Swallow is telling us something. Maybe it does belong here, after all.

Taking the Plunge

THE SUMMER'S GONE and the sap isn't rising any more. September just isn't sexy. The cold weather is coming and the heat is off. The birds' reproductive organs have shrivelled and the ardour of the breeding season has all but disappeared. Birds are in their resting phase, and they just aren't interested.

Do you believe that? Not a bit of it! Somehow that's just not the way of birds, is it, not those razor-sharp creatures we share our gardens with? Birds might be physically uninterested in reproduction at the moment, but not all of them have forgotten about the opposite sex. They never do.

Take ducks, for example. Maybe your garden pond is not big enough for them, but bear with me, will you, and take a trip to the park? If you watch the paddlers and dabblers carefully, there's a lot to see. It's subtle and it's understated, but ducks are red hot with lust at the moment, and you can tell if you know what to look for.

It's partly to do with the way in which ducks change their plumage. Male ducks don't just have a winter and a summer plumage; they have a breeding plumage, which is worn between September and the following July, and a moulting or 'eclipse' plumage worn for a brief time in the summer months. The fact is that drakes at the end of September are sporting a very new and very fine set of feathers, making them look dapper and colourful. They are wearing new suits, and the females love them.

Gesturing Flocks

The autumn, then, is a time when ducks often pair up. The pairs don't always hold together, and many individuals wait until the late winter or early spring before the serious stuff takes place. But the diminishing days from late September onwards see plenty of courtship displays upon the water, and the casual watcher can derive great fun and amusement from watching it all happen.

The delight of a Mallard's display is in its subtlety. Blink and you miss it; see it and you might still fail to recognise it. Sometimes a wink of an eye or the rub of an ear betrays the

attraction of human partners. Among ducks the small signs are the big signals, too.

So watch the males on the water, swimming around with the females in the hope of being fed some bread. Every so often one will flap its wings: exercise? No. Courtship? Yes. Another male might shake its head. It's another signal. Another might wag its tail, and again it is full of meaning.

We've all heard a Mallard quack, a series of noisy but diminishing nagging sounds like a belly laugh. Only the females do this. The males give the occasional wheezy effort, but they are not the real quackers. Instead, they have a high-pitched, quiet

In autumn several male Mallards may gather together to display to a single female.

whistle, sounding just a little like a sonar blip from a submarine. Among these gesturing flocks of Mallards the quiet whistle is another sign that the juices are flowing among the ducks as they paddle.

Sometimes the show is a little more obvious; Mallards make movements that cannot be mistaken for a stretch or an intention to fly. When the mood takes the males their movements become more elaborate. A male might put his bill to the water, then rear up and flick a shower of droplets into the air. Or he might, for no apparent reason, lift his tail slightly out of the water as well. It's common to see several males do this all at once, or several one after the other, each delivering their weak whistle to make a feeble chorus, like ringers of miniature bells in need of practice. This communal courtship may be

delivered by ten or more birds.

As yet, there is little seriousness in these pre-nuptial efforts. But every so often you will see a flight chase, in which a female will take off without warning, pursued by one or more males. This usually indicates a bit more interest from a female, a sign that, among a few of the Mallards at least, pairing will come early.

But most Mallards have a winter in front of them to perform their ceremonies and, in most years, plenty more talent is due to come down from Scandinavia for the colder months, and cause the usual furore among the Brits. The warmer days of early autumn are just the beginning. Only the harshest winter days, still far off, will dampen down the long-running antics of our sex-mad waterfowl.

AUTUMNALLY

speaking, September has been a dummy run; it's really a summer month in disguise. But now that October has arrived, the autumn speaks up as it should. Save for a few Swallows and martins flying over the house to an uncertain future, the summer migrants have departed. And rather than offering a few timid blushes, the leaves are turning shockingly red, and many – at last – are beginning to fall.

OCTOBER

Let's Get Together

IT'S THE HEART of Autumn, and most birds are now free agents. Apart from the various species that pair for the long term, all have shaken off any responsibilities towards a partner. All the children have left for ever. Individuals are not tied to dependants, nest or territory. For a few months at least, the only burden they will carry is themselves, and their only responsibility will be to their own survival.

One might expect the newly unfettered individuals to sigh with relief and keep themselves to themselves. But in fact, the reverse is true. October is a month when everyone seems to be going round in flocks. Far from being retiring, the majority of birds are suddenly sociable. Even in the garden, with a few notable exceptions such as Robins or Wrens, one can hardly see one bird without seeing another.

Starlings are always sociable, but their flocks become huge in October, with breeding adults mixing with the year's youngsters on lawns and playing-fields. The garden may also play host to a flock of Chaffinches, one moment mousy-brown on the ground, the next moment boldly black and white as they take off to the sanctuary of a low tree. Long-winged gulls pass over on their way from rubbish tips, suburbs and fields to their roosting sites on the coast or large lakes. All these birds and more find the end-of-season air ripe for conviviality.

In gardens, woods and hedgerows loose gatherings of birds of various species often form during the day. The core species are usually tits of various kinds, but Goldcrests, Treecreepers and other small species frequently join their ranks, too. The membership of such mixed-species flocks is relatively fluid: although some birds turn up each morning, probably at much the same time, and register their membership day after day, others appear to float around a considerable area and shift from group to group.

One of these mixed flocks passing through the garden is an engrossing sight. In autumn there could be anything between twenty and a hundred birds of four or five species. The different birds make for their chosen niches: Blue Tits to the tree canopy, Great Tits further down on thicker branches or on the ground, Long-tailed Tits halfway up and a Nuthatch, say, hugging the trunk. Each will spend a few seconds on a perch, grab a meal and move on, often to the opposite side of a tree, or to the next. The flock moves on like a column of arboreal ants, busy and never waiting. After a few minutes they will be lost to sight, and then only their calls can be heard, eventually fading.

Following the Crowd

This great move towards sociability asks an important question: what are flocks for? We know that flocking becomes feasible once birds are emancipated from their territories, but why not move around alone? It seems that there are two possible answers.

One answer could be that flocks are places of learning. By following the crowd, a bird might discover rich feeding areas it never knew about. When you wonder about this option, think about how any bird originally found your bird table: a few inquisitive souls would have stumbled upon it themselves, but the rest probably found it by tagging

Previous page: In October many garden birds go around in flocks.

Left: A feeding Starling checks for danger. By being in a flock, it will spend less time checking, and more time feeding.

October brings flocks of Redwings to the garden, seeking berries and thrown out fruit.

along behind others, like executives discovering a good restaurant. Finches, in particular, spend their lives looking for well-spaced food sources, such as clumps of thistles, seeding trees or weed-patches. More pairs of eyes must help them locate more food than birds working alone. And Goldfinches are especially intriguing in this respect. After a good feed in the morning, various groups of these birds have a habit of meeting together for a mutual preen and sing; during these 'coffee breaks' it seems likely that they are sharing information in some way. Plump and healthy birds may not point their less fortunate acquaintances towards a good thistle-bed, but their hearty demeanour may cause the others to follow them when they leave. Flocks observe flocks, and learn from the successful ones.

Within flocks of tits, individuals also probably observe their peers for instruction. An individual bird tends to survive by continuing to do something, or searching in a certain place, that has brought success in the past. By having other birds around, it can observe other techniques being successful, too. It can then try out new tricks for itself and add them to its repertoire.

But the learning element is only half the story, because flocks have another indisputable advantage as well: they promote the safety of each member. More pairs of eyes are bound to spot predators more efficiently. Why else would various species of birds tag along with tit parties, for example? A bird in a flock spends more time feeding, and less time looking up, than a bird on its own, knowing that when it is engrossed in foraging, someone else is bound to be alert.

With such advantages to be gained by seeking the company of others, it's not surprising that so many birds spend so much time in flocks. But of course, like an apparently irresistible offer one might receive in the post, there is a downside to it as well. That is that birds behave badly in flocks. They steal from weaker members and, more commonly, the stronger individuals take a disproportionate amount of the available food, keeping the others away from it with threats or physical attacks. Put kids in flocks and they do the same; the bigger, bullying ones grab most of the sweets for themselves.

In parties of birds, especially those that stay together long enough to get to know each other, there is inevitably a hierarchy, a 'pecking order' if you like. Typically, males are dominant over females, and older birds lord it over the younger element. There is also a similar hierarchy for the different species in mixed flocks. Those at the wrong end of a pecking order obtain the least food and are subject to the most disturbances. Those at the top end have a high old time, and grow fat at the expense of their inferiors. The weaker birds might do better on their own, if it were not for the mutual protection that they still gain from being flock members.

Among groups of Woodpigeons there is a particularly sinister twist to the dominance hierarchy in this respect. In larger groups on fields or wide lawns the dominant birds make sure that they stay in the middle of the feeding flock, and thereby force the weaker birds to the margins. Although the food towards the edge of the flock might be as rich, this is not a good place to be. The experienced Sparrowhawk or fox knows that birds at the centre of flocks are harder to catch than those on the outside; by means of their hierarchy, the pigeons ensure that the weak and young are available just where their executioners want them. Much the same sort of thing has happened among human armies throughout history: barely trained and youthful conscripts have been placed like sacrificial lambs at the front and sides of a line of troops, whilst the professional soldiers were stationed just behind them, ready for action after the initial, devastating hit.

You might read all this and say, fine, birds are in flocks in the autumn, but if that is so, where are all the flocks in my garden? I have birds at the feeders all the time, but only a few finches or tits are there at any one time, enough to count on the fingers of one hand. It's a typical observation and it's easy to assume that there are just a few birds in your area, but it's unlikely to be true. From now until the late spring, many of our favourite species, especially the tits, Chaffinches and Greenfinches, will tend to visit gardens in shifts, one gang after the other, spending a short time in each site before moving on elsewhere. They are creatures of habit, coming at the same time each day, plying a regular beat that may carry them several kilometres between dawn and dusk. After a day of visits from various gangs, even a small urban garden can expect between fifty and a hundred different individuals to have passed through.

There is one fairly common bird that you simply never see on its own, at any time of year, and that's the Long-tailed Tit. If you're fortunate enough to have these birds visiting you regularly, you'll know that they are confirmed socialites,

A Fieldfare pops in for a meal of berries.

forever in small parties. If one suddenly appears on the nuts or on a bush, the rest will soon appear, one after the other, flying with weak but rapid wing-beats to catch up their colleagues, tails trailing behind. They call to each other incessantly, with a piercing 'see-see-see-see' and become very agitated if they are left behind, even for a moment. These little parties may not look unusual or special, but it's the familiar that deceives. They are very special indeed.

Blood Relatives

What is unusual is the membership. Other flocks of garden birds are made up of strangers that might get to know each other over the course of time, might eventually form pairs, but harbour no genetic links. Long-tailed Tits, almost uniquely, consort with their blood relatives, and their flocks consist of birds that know each other intimately. Each group is built around a senior adult pair, and they are accompanied by their offspring from the breeding season just past. In addition to this family unit are a variable number of uncles and aunts, each one from the male's side of the family. These birds probably attempted to breed last season, but for one reason or another, failed to do so. Rather than kicking their heels, they went off to join their brother and help him at the nest. Their reward for their labour is to become a member of this flock, right from late summer and through to the following spring, gaining all the benefits that family flock membership confers.

October is the month when some sociable migrant birds, Redwings and Fieldfares, might first turn up in large numbers. Both are thrushes, and will spend the winter months roaming around the country in flocks looking for berries in the hedgerows and small animals on fields or in leaf litter. They both have an exotic look, the Redwing with russet under its wings and with a bold pale stripe over its eye, the Fieldfare with smoky-grey head and back, and smooth velvet back. And they are both very shy, taking flight at the slightest disturbance, away before you have adequate time to admire them. These two thrushes often visit gardens, and an October sighting of one of them is as much a part of the changing season as the last Swallow hurrying south.

In common with many other migrants, Redwings and Fieldfares tend to travel at night. So on any starry October evening, with frost in the air, go outside and listen hard, cupping your hands over the back of your ears and looking heavenward. Within a few minutes, whether you live in the country or in a large city, you are almost certain to hear the 'shack, shack' chuckle of the Fieldfare, or the high-pitched whistle 'seep' of the Redwing, as sharp as the cold. The thrill of autumn will grip you, and the wildness of the travellers you have just heard will remind you that a garden is not the tame place you might imagine it is at all.

Cache it While You Can – The Jay's Secret Larder

IF BIRDS HAD wishes, they must wish that the autumn lasted all year. Free at last from the responsibilities of bringing up young, the season gives them time to devote to themselves and to their own welfare. For once there is plenty of food around, and it's a doddle to find. What more could a bird ask for? If the autumn could be bottled, they would bottle it up and take a sip whenever they needed to.

It is not like that, of course. The autumn fades and its bounty fades with it. Berries shrivel on the trees and bushes, uneaten and sadly wasted, like a fortune squandered. Winter is autumn's creditor, and soon almost everything is lost.

But what if it could be stored and kept for later? What an advantage that would be. If somehow some of the autumn overproduction could be put aside for a rainy day, future survival could be almost guaranteed.

And of course, with such huge theoretical benefits attached, it will come as no surprise that there are several birds in the garden that have tapped into this possibility, collecting food supplies and storing them away for the long term. The best known of them, and by far the most obvious, is the Jay, that four-colour crow that sometimes arrives ghost-like upon our feeding trays, causing all the small birds to scatter.

The Jay bottles autumn by collecting its output of acorns. Acorns are tough, long-lasting fruits, ideal for leaving in a safe place, hidden away, without the fear that they will spoil. So the Jays collect them in huge numbers, from late

A Jay carries away an acorn in its bill. At the same time, another two will probably be carried in the bird's gullet.

September to early November every year.

And during this time, the normally secretive Jay is suddenly everywhere, flying over gardens, car parks, railway lines and motorways, out in the open, seemingly always on the move. And there's a reason for this. In autumn, few Jays have access to their own oak tree, so instead they must commute each day to reach them. Leaving the garden briefly, they go to the nearest oak wood, collect what acorns they can, and bring them back to secrete away within their own borders. And they do this again and again. Over the course of the season, each Jay stashes away about five thousand acorns in all.

It must be an exhausting job. The nearest suitable oak trees may be several kilometres away. The Jays must fly to them, find the acorns and then pick up as many as they can comfortably hold for the return flight (an average load is three, carried in the crop and gullet, although as many as nine is possible). After this they must hide away their acorns, one at a time. They cannot store them all away in one site, because that would be courting disaster – just one break-in by a miscreant

127

squirrel would waste all their hard work.

It only takes about five minutes to arrive at a site and collect the required load, so the visits are brief and the birds are quickly on their way back to their own territory. Once inside their boundaries and on familiar ground, one might expect that their next task, hiding the loot, would be easy. But in fact it isn't; it can take as many as fifteen minutes just to dispense the three acorns. Think of it: where would you hide five thousand acorns in your garden and another twenty adjoining ones? After the first few efforts, it must get pretty tricky.

A Savings Account

Nonetheless, as the days pass, the territory's nooks and crannies fill up. In general, every acorn is stored in isolation, under leaf-litter, or roots, or sticks, or in the ground. They might be squeezed between the fissures of bark, or in tree boles, or at the junction of branch forks. Wherever the fruits might have a chance to escape detection, the Jay stores them. The process is not slapdash. An acorn buried in the ground is truly hidden, covered first with soil and then with litter or other detritus. The bird uses its bill as a trowel, moving the earth where it needs to go with a fastidious flourish.

The Jay's overall larder is a little like a savings account; one way to look at it is that each bird puts five thousand items of its currency into the bank, enough to last the winter. A Jay will not need to

uncover a cache every day because, as an omnivore, it has plenty of options of other food, not least from the bird table. But some days will bring less reward than others, especially if the weather is bad, and those are the days when a Jay will need to seek out its secret larder. Using its excellent long-term memory, it appears to be able to re-find a considerable proportion of its hiding places, using landmarks on the ground or in the trees. There is even a record of a Jay digging through a foot of snow to find its allocation on a fierce winter day.

The Jay, then, is a wise investor. It snatches a bit of autumn and hides it away for a rainy day. It's not completely reliant on this cache, but withdraws modestly, a little at a time, and only when it is in severe need. If any people were to manage their resources this way, they would undoubtedly soon be rich.

Jays invest for the long term, too, in a way that is beneficial to many subsequent generations. When several thousand items are hidden away, some inevitably end up overlooked or unwanted. These 'lost' acorns, buried safely in the ground, quite naturally follow nature's course, set seed, and begin to grow. Years later, the forgotten fruits are mighty oaks, serving the Jays of the future.

And that, in a way, is like taking autumn's potion, and bottling it for ever.

Made for Each Other – Birds and Berries

IT'S AUTUMN, AND the trees and shrubs are feeling generous. Their branches are stacked with berries, full to overflowing like opulent supermarket shelves. Drawn irresistibly, the berry-eating customers are many, and their shopping days are long. No one goes away from the sales dissatisfied.

Visit any berry-bearing tree in October, and you can see the enthusiasm of the birds as they come and go and quarrel over the fruits. But who is the chief beneficiary of this plundering? True, the birds are stuffing themselves like Romans at a feast, their tummies are full and their engines are being renewed - the berries give their consumers carbohydrate, and bags of energy, and a means to put on weight. But what of the plant, which has devoted so much energy into making the best-selling products? When a bird eats a berry it digests the pulp and ejects the seeds in its faeces, thereby dispersing the seeds to places where they may germinate and a new plant can grow. The berries service the birds and the birds distribute the plants; everyone benefits.

Mass Appeal

As with all products intended for 'sale', berries come in a variety of styles and types to suit their customers. Some are red, some are black, some are yellow and a few are white. The red and yellow ones are designed to appeal to the masses: birds, having colour vision, can hardly fail to notice them against the green background of foliage. The black ones are less obvious to us, but there is evidence that some have ultraviolet reflectance which is easily picked up by particular species. The white berries are a speciality item, taken by just a few devotees such as Mistle Thrushes. All berries look succulent, and many are just the right size for their intended dispersers. In contrast to flowers they are essentially odourless, suggesting that their appeal is not primarily to the dispersers that are led by the nose, such as small mammals, but to birds only. And there is a berry for every taste.

The different birds have their favourites. Redwings, for example, which are small thrushes, tend to take the smaller varieties of berry such as hollies and haws; the Mistle Thrush, a really big member of the family, prefers sloes, because they are larger and offer a more substantial meal.

But it's not all to do with size and shape: the Fieldfare, another nomadic winter visitor like the Redwing, is a fussy eater, going only for holly, rose hips, haws and, later in the winter, for ivy. In contrast the Blackbird, famous opportunist that it is, will eat almost any berry at all. With so much fruit of so many kinds available, birds can afford to be selective.

The Blackcap is one of the smaller birds that eats berries.

Although thrushes are often the most noticeable berry-eaters, there are plenty of others. Starlings, for example, treat fruit as a fad; they take it in vast quantities at some times of the year, as if it had just been recommended by a famous TV cook, but ignore it for the remainder. In October they can be seen attacking elderberries in hordes, treating the fruit-eating as a highly sociable event. They also attack blackberries, like human out-of-towners getting a feel for the produce of the countryside.

Some fruit-eaters are more secretive. Have you ever seen a Robin plucking fruit, for example? Although highly aggressive, the Robin is a small bird, and must approach a bush carefully to avoid attack by a larger berry eater; its favourite tipple is elder, although it's also partial to ivy. The Blackcap is another species that goes undercover, skulking around elder or holly in true warbler fashion and keeping its mouth shut. The secretive brigade may be less obvious, but they are performing the same valuable service to the plant as their more demonstrative counterparts.

The exotic looking Waxwing is the only British bird that eats nothing but fruit in the winter.

Most fruit-eaters cannot rely on fruit alone for their nutriment. Berries are carbohydrate-rich and great for a surge of energy, but they lack protein; the wise bird must add a sprinkling of invertebrate meals to its autumn diet. But one bird is an exception to this rule, the Waxwing. Exotically clad in silky colours, this is a rare and treasured visitor from the north, only turning up in Britain in significant numbers every decade or so. It is a specialist fruit-eater, or 'frugivore', with a wide gape for swallowing lots of different kinds of berries, and it seems to get by on this food source alone, although nobody as yet knows how. It certainly eats berries in enormous quantities: Waxwings

have been known to eat a thousand cotoneaster fruits a day.

The Waxwing's passion for berries has created a curious birdwatching anomaly. In the last ten years or so, the pernicious spread of the out-of-town shopping centre has brought some small environmental compensation in the form of the attached car parks being landscaped with berry-bearing shrubs. They are an ideal food source for many frugivorous birds, including Waxwings, and the northern invaders seem to be recorded in this strange alien landscape more than anywhere else. The birds are so gorgeous, with their exotic plumage and rarity value, that along with the Waxwing influxes there is a concomitant increase in bird-mad members of households volunteering to do the shopping.

Dispersers and Predators

For the cotoneasters concerned, the gobbling Waxwings are offering them a thousand opportunities for bird-borne dispersal each day, at least in theory. That's the beauty of the bird-berry relationship. The more the one is satisfied, the more the other is satisfied. Birds and berries are made for each other.

Still, nothing is ever simple in the natural world, not in gardens or anywhere else. The bird/berry relationship may be mutually beneficial, but it is subject to cheating. And it's the birds, unfortunately, that do it. They ruin the agreement by being attracted to the berries, but actually eating the seeds inside them. The cycle is broken, and the seeds are not distributed. Some birds are not seed dispersers, but seed predators. Quite a few seed predators live in the garden, among them tits, finches and Woodpigeons. Greenfinches and Blue Tits chew away at rose hips, and Woodpigeons – easily seen and caught in the act – munch ivy berries. Seeds are more nutritious than berries, you see. It is not surprising that some species abuse the arrangement.

But seed-predators that target berries are fewer in number than the seed dispersers. That's just as well for the legions of the latter. Otherwise it would not be long before the plants got wind of the birds' impertinence, and ceased to produce their luscious fruits. That would deprive the birds of an important food source, and drastically change the autumnal look of both the garden and the countryside.

Store Stories

ALTHOUGH THE JAY is by far the most obvious food-storing bird in the garden, flying back and forth with its acorns in full view of everyone, it is not the only one. Other birds practise the strategy too, but on different resources and often in different ways.

The Nuthatch has the closest game plan to the Jay's. This long-billed, tree-hugging bird lives in a territory all year round, much as the Jay does, and spends countless hours of the autumn collecting excess food supplies and hiding them away for the long-term. It collects various types of nuts, including acorns, and wedges them among fissures of bark, or even in holes in walls. In common with the Jay the Nuthatch is a scatter-hoarder, secreting each item away separately to prevent a single disastrous break-in by a competitor. It covers many of its hidden seeds with pieces of bark or moss, leaving little evidence of its activity.

Scatter-hoarding for the long term requires formidable powers of memory recall, and it also calls for the right kind of material to be stored. Several members of the crow family, including Magpies, Rooks and Carrion Crows are also given to hoarding, but will also cache perishable items that must be removed within a day or two. The Magpie, for example, has been recorded hiding away the half-eaten bodies of birds and mammals, and the Carrion Crow appears partial to burying animal faeces in the ground: how a dog-owner would relish such a helper for this tiresome task!

The Magpie has a well-established reputation for taking away items that catch its eye, such as wedding rings, coins and other items, enough to give rise to the expression 'The Thieving Magpie'. When it does pick up these inanimate objects, it must be something of a let-down for the bird to find that they are inedible. However, one particular Magpie that hit the headlines recently found a unique use for its spoils: it learnt to look for dropped coins and deliver them to an entrepreneurial bird gardener in return for morsels of food!

Covert Operations

If you watch the comings and goings of the bird table closely, you will probably notice that the Coal Tit never stays very long when it visits. Instead it makes off with a nut as soon as it has acquired it, as if it were a robber dashing away from a store detective. This is because the Coal Tit is another food-storer. A well-stocked bird table is equivalent to a big find of seeds on the forest floor. Rather than wait and let all its competitors deplete the supply, it acquires what it can when it can, in a fit of panic buying.

The Coal Tit's stores don't last for long, usually just a few days at the most. If they are left longer, the owner apparently forgets about them. What the Coal Tit is responding to is not its long-term needs, but the repressive regime of the dominant Blue Tits and Great Tits. Caching is simply a method of acquiring extra food from under the noses of the blue and yellow uniforms of the garden's police authorities.

If your garden is particularly fortunate you might be visited regularly by a less common, smart-capped tit, the Marsh Tit – a bird that, despite its name, avoids marshes altogether. The food-storing of this bird has been

Like the Jay, the Nuthatch is a "scatter hoarder," secreting a great many items away in dozens of hiding places.

The Marsh Tit is an inveterate storer of food, and a clever one, too.

particularly well studied. In addition to seeds, it stores small invertebrates, too, including decapitated caterpillars, aphids and even tiny slugs. The aphids are often stored in little balls mixed in with the bird's saliva. It usually stores food in the morning, and retrieves it in the afternoon.

Marsh Tits, which also live under repression from Blue and Great Tits, are apparently very selective about where they store their food, and certain individuals have preferred sites. Some favour the grass, some hide food away in moss, others scrabble among the leaf litter. But, being intelligent birds, they change their preferences every few days, switching to new hiding places as soon as there is a hint that the bully-boys are getting wind of their undercover activities. Marsh Tits also have exceptional recall, remembering a high proportion of their hiding places for a period of up to three days.

The Undercover Army

HAVE YOU LOOKED closely at the birds in your garden recently? Do you think you could recognise them as your own? Is the Blackbird feeding on your lawn the very same one that nested in your hedge last summer? If you think you can tell, you might be in for a shock.

When most people think of migration, the picture in their mind's eye is almost inevitably of a Swallow or Cuckoo making its way, against the odds, to its winter home in Africa. But what might surprise many is that, to millions of birds from northern and eastern Europe, Britain is, in fact, the equivalent of Africa. For Serengeti savannah, swap a lawn in Milton Keynes. To a bird seeking suitable wintering grounds there's little difference.

Britain, being on the western fringe of continental Europe, has its winter climate mollified by the Gulf Stream. On the whole we do not have long periods of snow cover, or the continuous frost that afflicts so much of central and northern Europe in the cold season. Our ponds, rivers and seas remain relatively ice-free. To an army of birds, that's all they need for winter survival. They hop across the Channel in October and November to our chilly but damp idyll, and end their journey here.

And most of these birds have familiar faces. They are foreigners, but not recognisably so.

Although some belong to species that don't breed commonly here, such as Redwings, Fieldfares or Bramblings, the vast majority do not stand out from their British counterparts in any obvious way. So it is that our gardens and countryside are flooded by incoming Blackbirds, Chaffinches, Goldcrests, Song Thrushes, Robins, Starlings, Black-headed Gulls and Woodpigeons, all of which are non-British EU nationals. They come from such places as Poland, Germany, Norway, Sweden, Estonia, France and Iceland.

The result of this invasion is that our sacred fields play host each winter to a pan-European gaggle of unregistered immigrants, each, presumably, determined to communicate in their own language. The more right-wing politicians would have a fit if they knew.

So watch out in your garden for these visitors. You can sometimes recognise them by their habit of coming in bulk; suddenly you have a flock of Chaffinches where before there were two individuals, or you have half a dozen Song Thrushes or Blackbirds in a previously private hedge. Many are nomads and will depart in a day or two; others will stay for the whole season. By March and April they will melt away, grateful for your provision and bidding you 'Auf Wiedersehen'.

Familiar garden Blackbirds – or are they? Many of your garden mainstays may actually be foreign nationals.

AFTER THE upheaval of the last few months, November brings a little order to the lives of birds in the garden. With winter around the corner, the emphasis shifts towards settling down. By the middle of the month, most faces in the garden are those that will become familiar over the next weeks and months.

NOVEMBER

Knives of the Long Night

NOVEMBER NEVER SEEMS to settle, as if it had some identity crisis. Its weather is schizophrenic, the two seasons of autumn and winter battling. Any November will see gentle days, when the sun politely brushes aside the early morning mist, and lights up the last and most vibrant autumn colour - the leaves having a last hurrah before they finally fall. Yet on other days those same leaves can be ripped down by violent winds, and be lashed where they lie by endless fits of rain. From start to finish, this month never seems to decide what its role is, and the birds must cope with it all.

Mist and fog are seldom a problem for birds, unless they are trying to travel somewhere. But rain is, especially when it's borne on lively winds. Although raindrops don't damage birds, heavy rain can be a physical barrier to activity: how many birds, for example, does one see on an uncovered bird table in a downpour? And although most birds are also well able to cope with getting slightly wet because their plumage is covered with preen-oil (which generally has excellent waterproofing properties) a really severe soaking can be dangerous. Rain also interferes with feeding areas, washing seeds from plants and disturbing bare soil. And it makes the harvesting of the diminished insect population almost impossible, the raindrops causing the invertebrates themselves to hide, and camouflaging their movements against the shaking of twigs or leaves.

Wind, especially of the irritating, shifting type, brings its own problems. For example, it can be hard for a bird to perch comfortably to keep look-out in a strong breeze, or to cling on to a seed-head. Wind also ruffles the plumage, disturbing the insulating layer of air that keeps a bird warm. And winds make a noise, potentially affecting a bird's ability to hear prey or predators. Wind and rain are not lethal in themselves, but many days of their influence can cause a bird to forage less effectively and lose condition. Such weakness is no basis from which to withstand the increasingly difficult weeks ahead.

Full Tanks

In November the birds are beginning to face a far more daunting and relentless challenge than the changing weather: the return of the shortest days and longest nights. After months when daytime activities have been dominating a bird's agenda, the emphasis now shifts towards surviving the hours of darkness. The equation familiar from January resurfaces: to stay alive, a bird must obtain enough food by day to fuel the long night. If not, the knives are out.

As they did at the beginning of the year, most garden birds, especially the smaller ones, spend more and more of the day feeding. In the gentler times of autumn, a Coal Tit will spend eighty per cent of its waking hours busy with foraging, but that percentage creeps up throughout November and December to about ninety per cent by the end of the year. They also increase the length of their working days, rising earlier and roosting later in relation to the dawn and dusk than they did in the summer.

Just about everybody also puts a special effort in towards evening to make sure that their tanks are full for the night. So those last minutes of light see a peak of activity. Pigeons go to bed with a full crop, and so do many finches. The crop contains undigested stores in addition to those that have been completely consumed, so throughout the night, individuals of these groups can wake up when they need to and have their own version of a midnight feast.

One finch in particular, the Redpoll, is notably sophisticated in this respect. It has a small pocket in its gullet, just below the neck, known by the grandiose title of an 'oesophageal diverticulum'. A bit like the pouches in a hamster's cheeks, the diverticulum provides a place where the bird can store that little extra bit of food neutrally to keep its dinner fires burning through the night. These birds also help their cause by adopting a ball-like shape when sleeping, with their feathers fluffed up as insulation from the cold. The belly feathers cover the legs and feet like a blanket, and the bill is similarly tucked away.

As we know from long-distance migrants, birds are also perfectly capable of storing fat reserves in their bodies, and, not surprisingly, they often do so to help them through the night: a small bird might store a tenth of its body weight, for example. But they cannot store too much, or they will be fatally slowed down if threatened by danger. They might get away with this for a few nights in theory, but night after night their

On cold nights, Wrens roost together in any sheltered hollow they can find. A nestbox is ideal.

chance of being captured greatly increases.

But it's not only gathering the required food that rides high in a bird's agenda for night-time survival. It must also find a suitable place to roost. A good roost site is like gold dust; it is essential for a bird's survival, just as much as reliable food. The site must be safe and sheltered, and, for most birds it must also be private, like a territory. Although there haven't been many observations of birds fighting over roosts, such is their importance that it must happen regularly, with serious consequences to the losers.

Sleeping Together

Roost-sites come in many forms. Nest-boxes are perfect for the task, and are highly sought after, just as they are in the spring; their commonest occupants are Great Tits, which probably oust the smaller species. Hedges, the thicker the better, are also ideal, and have Blackbirds, Robins and Dunnocks sheltering in their mass of vegetation. Climbers such as ivy and Virginia creeper have the advantage of being close to a hard surface, such as a tree trunk or a wall, affording added shelter: Wrens, Robins and House Sparrows use these. Shrubs, especially of cypress, are particularly popular with Greenfinches and other finches. Trees attract pigeons and crows. Even outbuildings such as sheds and greenhouses will have their own opportunistic squatters. So long as there is shelter, birds will sleep there.

Although most birds have to look for a suitable site for sleeping, some build their own dormitories.

Woodpeckers, not surprisingly, sleep in holes that they have excavated themselves. House Sparrows build special nests, often near or on street lights and other sources of heat. And Treecreepers seek out Wellingtonia trees: these giants have such soft bark that even needle-billed insectivores can rough out a small hollow into which they can cling and flatten their bodies out of the wind. But surprisingly few birds actually construct a place where they can safely rest. Perhaps this is because it takes so much effort out of a day when foraging is a more sensible occupation. There might also be competition. Building a nest for roosting will take energy, which will be grievously wasted if another bird comes and usurps the site before the builder can benefit.

Several of our garden birds forsake the privacy of their nights to roost communally, in large or small groups. Blackbirds, pigeons, Starlings, Pied Wagtails and crows are among them, and so is the exotic Ring-necked Parakeet, an Indian bird that has been introduced to several parts of the country, including London. Communal roosts are often spectacular to watch, and inevitably noisy. Blackbirds make angry 'chink, chink' calls as each tries to settle down. Crows caw angrily; Starlings make an incessant communal squeal which lasts the whole night. Only pigeons keep their counsel; just the occasional staccato wing-flaps are heard.

One might imagine that most birds that sleep in company with others are doing so in order to benefit from an extra bit of body warmth, just as human mountaineers share sleeping bags on the coldest bivouacs when they are stranded. But this isn't so. A Blackbird entering a roost site is like a passenger embarking on a London Underground tube train: if the carriage is almost empty, he or she will find the least occupied part and sit there, avoiding the taboo practice of sitting next to a stranger. The same applies to birds. Being in close bodily contact is stressful, and is avoided where possible.

Information Centres

So why, then, should they sleep near to each other? The answer to this is far from clear. If it's not for warmth, then the next suggestion would be safety. But large roosts attract predators – predators aren't stupid, after all – and the birds make no effort at all to conceal themselves. A big roost would theoretically reduce a bird's chances of being caught (since there are more birds around, the likelihood of being the unlucky bird diminishes), but this could easily be offset by the sheer numbers of bird-eaters attending the roost for an easy meal. Overall, it's hard to see safety as the complete answer.

More recently, the idea of large roosts as information and learning centres has gained ground. It's an interesting idea. As everybody comes into the 'hotel' each evening, the other guests automatically monitor their condition and see if they've had a good day's feeding - and if they have, they will be well worth following the next morning.

But if that is so, what's in it for the successful birds in going back to the hotel? What's to stop them roosting alone, keeping their rich feeding grounds secret? The answer here probably does lie in personal safety. A roost is indeed like a hotel: some rooms are very much better than others, more sheltered, more comfortable, safer. If a successful bird benefits from being in a large roost, in that it has a wide buffer zone between it and the more dangerous margins of the roost, it will be perfectly willing to sacrifice a bit of its know-how the following day.

In fact communal roosts are subject to the same rules of hierarchy as daytime flocks. If a lot of birds sleep together in one tree or bush, there is much jostling at bedtime for the best positions. Clearly some perches will be more sheltered than others, and these are occupied by the dominant birds, whilst the subordinates, as ever, are marginalised.

A particularly interesting example of how roosts reflect the hierarchy is shown by Rooks.

Pied Wagtails roost in groups and have a special "summoning call" to draw colleagues in from the surrounding area.

These crows sleep in large trees, not the ones where they build their rookeries, but in others nearby. Birds travel miles to these favoured sites to roost in large numbers, and the Rooks are often joined by Jackdaws. With so many bodies packed close together, each having recently digested a heavy evening meal, it is the practice of the dominant birds to take the highest perches on the trees, away from the shower of faeces that falls on the lower branches every night. But if the night is windy, the positions change. The wind diverts some of the faeces away, making the lower perches a cleaner option. But better than this, the lower perches are more sheltered and warmer, a perfect place for a dominant Rook. The oft-bespattered subordinates are condemned to the chilly heights.

Cuddler by Nature

Some winter nights are so cold that the elegant theories of communal roosting are tossed away, and the members of a roost do indeed knuckle down in physical contact in order to benefit from their shared body heat. In snowy or frosty conditions, even highly strung Wrens gather in small spaces to sleep alongside their congeners, much as human street people may retreat to a hostel on the very worst nights. It is not their normal practice; they much prefer to roost alone. But in fear of their lives Wrens cuddle together, sometimes in several layers in a confined space, with each bird facing inward. It must be uncomfortable and stressful, but the survival value of such hostels must be high. Sixty-one Wrens have been known to use a single nest-box, packed together like sardines.

Although Wrens adopt the huddle as an extreme measure, there is one garden bird that is a cuddler by nature: the Long-tailed Tit. Every night these sociable birds select a perch and sit side by side, their bodies touching, all facing one way, tails trailing down, like a row of lollipops on a sweet rack. The dominant birds hog the centre, while the various subordinates take the outer positions. The usual stress of being in bodily contact is ameliorated by the fact that the birds know each other intimately. They are blood relatives and see each other every day.

A Long-tailed Tit flock, remember, consists of a senior male and female, their most recently fledged young, and a number of aunts and uncles related to the senior male. The aunts and uncles don't just appear in the autumn and apply to join the flock. They must earn their way in, and do so by helping their brother with feeding his young during the breeding season, assuming that their own nesting attempt has failed. They are, if you like, members of an extended family that holds together throughout the summer and autumn. There is little doubt that their efforts during breeding greatly enhance the current year's brood's survival. And there is little doubt, too, that the survival value of the huddle is such that they would soon perish without it.

That begs a question. If it is so imperative that an individual Long-tailed Tit finds a flock with which to huddle at night that its life depends on it, could that be the reason that failed breeders help their siblings to bring up their young in the first place, with all the effort that that entails? If so, it is perhaps not so surprising. Birds will do almost anything to avoid the knives of the long night.

Very few birds go to sleep in bodily contact with others, but Long-tailed Tits do.

The Starling's Sleeping Habits

IT'S EARLY AFTERNOON on a November day, the light will soon be fading, and something remarkable is about to happen. The Starlings are about to go to roost.

In gardens everywhere gangs of these streetwise birds halt their jaunty marches across the lawn and decide that it's time to fly back towards the site where they encountered the dawn. Each flock rises as one and makes for the nearest rooftops, where its members loaf and sing for a moment and then move off, triangular wings flapping, along the suburban commuter line.

At the same time as the human city workers are leaving the urban centre after a day at their desks, the Starlings are going in the opposite direction. After being in the country or suburbs, the Starlings know that a town or city may offer slightly warmer night air than the wider countryside, and they are prepared to fly fifty kilometres (30 miles) or more to get there. But if urban centres are too far away, they will make for a convenient sheltered spot with thick bushes, or reedbeds, or dense, low conifers. As everybody travels towards the roost, flocks join up with flocks like commuter carriages filling up, and the small gatherings become large ones as the birds stream in, all making for the same place. Built up from units of a dozen or so working the outlying gardens and neighbourhoods, the flocks may number thousands as they close in towards their own mainline station, where they will alight and await the darkness. The station is not their final destination. The Starlings are like football supporters arriving for a match. First they arrive in all directions at the stadium's station and then travel, en masse, to the pitch-side itself. For now they remain in their pre-roost assembly, excited multitudes awaiting the last stage.

In the moments before sunset the pre-roost assembly is a place of great energy and motion – the birds are not contemplating sleep just yet. Instead they preen, drink, bicker, and feed – another parallel with their human counterparts.

Somehow – and no one knows how – the word is given, and the assembled birds all take to the air. They will now do one of two things: either they will fly straight to the roost site and settle; or they will remain airborne and indulge in some mass aerobatics. The latter is an extraordinary aerial demonstration, possibly aimed at others of their kind, to invite them to the roost. With every Starling giving voice, thousands fly back and forth across the sky again and again, swooping low, or gaining height, circling or flying straight, every bird or group seemingly doing its own thing, yet giving the effect of a single, large-scale choreographed manoeuvre. From a distance the giant flocks resemble smoke swirling in the wind, sometimes gently puffing, at other times catching the wind. Further back still the flock seems to take on the appearance of one huge organism languishing in the sky. Against the setting sun the multitudes heave back and forth for minutes on end, until their forms begin to fade against the darkening sky. Then the invisible signal is given to end their exuberant aerial evolutions, and they stream dutifully to the rooftops to settle in.

Starlings are restless birds, by day and by night. With so many individuals jostling for the best positions, peace does not come to the roost quickly: it is more like a dormitory of excited children than an army camp full of exhausted squaddies. It is doubtful, whether the birds get much sleep at all. In the November darkness conversation babbles on all night long.

By dawn every bird, whether it has had a nap or not, is fully awake. The chattering of the night becomes a murmur and then a roar as each individual finds its voice and has its say about the new day.

Looking like drifting smoke, a great flock of Starlings gathers to roost on Brighton's West Pier.

As dawn breaks a mass of Starlings looks disorganised, but the birds are about to leave in a highly disciplined rota.

Many birds have an early morning preen, and some shuffle around, giving their wings some exercise. There is a great waking up, and a yawn and a stretch. It will soon be time to move off.

When you see Starlings at a bird feeder gobbling food down with unedifying haste, quarrelling over scraps and generally making a nuisance of themselves, it's tempting to conclude that their species is an undisciplined creature. Yet in the semi-darkness of a gigantic roost at dawn, the Starlings show such organisation that this charge could not possibly be levelled at them. In a few moments they will confound their critics and their reputation. An extraordinary staggered departure, as regimented as the best army drill, is about to get underway.

Inside the roost the volume builds up as the birds sing, and the sound of many thousands of squeaky voices fills the city air. It comes from all corners and yet, when some unknown signal is given, the whole roost falls quiet for a second, and a few birds fly around before quickly landing again. Another burst of song follows, reaching a crescendo until, once again the birds fall silent and a few cards in the pack are shuffled. A third time the song builds up, and yet again silence suddenly falls. But now more birds fly up and around, and circle the roost site, not landing but getting their bearings. They circle the area again and then, in small groups, head off in all directions.

The remaining birds – still by far the majority at the roost – start up their singing once more in approval. Yet again there is a huge crescendo and yet again, no surprise, another brief silence. This is the cue for the second exodus, and many hundreds of birds circle around and once again go off in small flocks to all corners of the lightening sky.

With two departures already gone, the drill becomes obvious and stereotyped: song, silence, circling and setting off. The body of the roost becomes smaller until, with the final silent cue, the last of its limbs flies off for the day. The body will re-form a few hours later, but for now the rooftops, reed tops or bush tops where it assembled are silent, except for the roar of traffic or wind.

The exodus of Starlings in the morning from their night time roost is a marvel of discipline and precision. The staggered departures have been measured by scientists, and each flight takes place about three minutes after the last. A truly large roost may have ten outbound flights and last for about half an hour. It is tempting to draw a parallel with the mainline station again, with commuter trains leaving for different places at three-minute intervals. The organisation required to get such a pattern working is difficult enough for electronically minded modern man, let alone these birds with their limited brains.

And it's all done to help the Starlings get their bare minimum of fitful sleep.

Fly by Night
– The Shadowy Life of the Tawny Owl

THE NIGHTS ARE getting longer, life is getting tougher, and one bird doesn't mind at all. It's the Tawny Owl, the garden's night-time master of ceremonies. As the hours of darkness increase, so its hunting opportunities are proliferating. It has little fear of the coming winter.

Go out into the garden at night in the blackness of November, and you can dip into the owl's domain. The shadows of the garden give it an unfamiliar feel, the same strangeness that a coating of deep snow gives to a well-trodden patch of land. You are disoriented and out of your depth. You could not begin to cope with the endless darkness.

And yet, curiously, the eyes of an owl are not much better than those of a human being, despite what many of us have come to believe. They are large, of course, and an owl can see very much better in the dark than other birds can. But essentially, whatever you yourself can see when your eyes get accustomed to the dark is what a Tawny Owl has to work on; the same shadows and darkness and mystery.

Where every owl defeats any human being is in its hearing, for owls, at their core, are birds that live and kill by sound, not sight. Some species can catch prey in total darkness, pinpointing them accurately with three-dimensional aural detection. They can tell what quarter a rustle is coming from by detecting the slight difference in time it takes for the same sound to reach each of their well-spaced ears, and they can also home in by registering differences in the intensity of the sound. And whatever they hear is funnelled towards the ear openings by their flat facial discs, the stiff feathers that give owls their wide-cheeked look. As it is funnelled the sound is magnified, an effect a little like putting your cupped hands behind your ears. Altogether, one might say that the garden's conversations are thoroughly tapped.

A Tawny Owl is not an especially energetic hunter. For much of a calm night it will sit on an elevated perch and listen for clues below on the ground. If anything moves it will glide down towards it, and grab it in its assassin's talons. But while waiting it must regularly shift perches. The profile of the garden changes with the hours, with certain prey becoming active at different times and in different places throughout the night.

But wherever an owl hunts, it is in familiar territory. A young bird's most urgent task upon leaving its parents' care is to find a patch of ground of its own. It will settle here and, over the months and years will get to know every corner. It will soon discover which birds roost in which trees, bushes or holes and where the small mammals hide; and it will know every possible source of food, mapping out the possibilities in its brain. If your garden has a Tawny Owl, it is perfectly possible that it knows your acreage far better than you, and has been in residence longer. Tawny Owls may live for ten or twenty years.

The Tawny Owl is the commonest of its kind to be found in gardens and woodland, occurring everywhere from urban centres to the most remote depths of deep forest. Its success derives mainly from its adaptability in habitat, and willingness to eat almost everything. No Tawny Owl is fussy about its food.

Catholic Diet

If it has been wet recently, expect a Tawny Owl to land upon your lawn at some time in the night. The owl is not too proud to eat earthworms, and will contentedly feast on them in great numbers. Worms are one of the few food items that a Tawny Owl will catch in its bill, standing on the ground listening for movement and then bounding forward to grab a wriggling body, like an ungainly Blackbird. At certain times an owl's night will be filled with worming expeditions on the local turf: availability is the key.

There is plenty of evidence, too, that Tawny Owls take fish from garden ponds at night. They catch them when they surface, either swooping down and plucking them from the air, or standing in the shallows getting their feet wet. If you've lost fish recently you have probably blamed a Heron, but who knows what the darkness brings?

Tawny Owls terrorise birds, and they are merciless in their attacks. Roost sites are at a

A full moon can help, but Tawny Owls hunt more by sound than by sight.

premium for the birds of the day, and a Tawny Owl's intelligence is good; it will probably know where they all are. Starlings, those restless sleepers, are a favourite target, the Tawny Owl simply diving into the bushes where they sleep. Individuals have been seen brushing foliage with their wings in order to flush sleeping birds out, catching them in their panic and disorientation. Other observers have claimed to have heard wing-claps used for the same purpose, much as we might clap when we are trying to chivvy pigeons from our feeding trays. Whatever the method, the result is the same; a feathered body is brought to a high perch for plucking.

Furry Creatures

The Tawny Owls of woodland specialise in catching wood mice, which are small, gentle creatures that make a handy snack. Garden Tawnies catch the wood mouse's equivalent in size, house mice, but they also tackle larger, more aggressive furry creatures near houses and by outbuildings: rats. To us rats are dirty and repellent, but to a Tawny Owl a rat is a large, wholesome meal, the kind of delicacy to make its

night worthwhile. Another sumptuous meal, and another killing that is likely to be enjoyed as much by the garden owner as the owl, is the Grey Squirrel. The Tawny Owls usually catch the inexperienced youngsters, reducing by one the bushy-tailed competition on the bird table next day.

There is only one blot on a Tawny Owl's dark horizon, and that is excess noise. Being hearing specialists with sensitive ears, owls find life difficult when it is raining hard or the wind is strong. They seem to be able to adapt to traffic noise, with its relatively low frequencies, but the rustle of leaves by the wind masks any telltale whisperings by a small body, and a stormy night must bring the hunters great frustration. Nevertheless, most territories probably contain a few sheltered places where it is peaceful enough for a spot of emergency hunting, enabling the owl to see out the storm.

By night the Tawny Owl is the garden's supreme avian predator. Few small living bodies, from insects to squirrels, are safe from its all-pervading reach. Living in the shadows has brought it success, a success borne of a number of special adaptations for detecting prey. The Tawny Owl is a fly-by-night, to be sure, but one that has admirable qualities.

143

The Case of the Disappearing Song Thrush

IN THE LAST fifty years a much-loved voice has broadcast from fewer treetops in Britain. The fabulous proclamations of the Song Thrush, those crystal clear and slightly urgent, perfectly enunciated repetitions, have become a less pervasive pleasure in our gardens. As the Song Thrush might itself declare it: 'The Song Thrush, the Song Thrush, the Song Thrush; is in trouble, trouble, trouble, trouble. Oh dear, oh dear, oh dear, oh dear!'

Long-term Decline

November marks the beginning of the singing season for our smallest widespread breeding thrush. It is a garden resident all year round, hugging the borders and undergrowth in a largely secret search for insects and snails, but occasionally sharing the lawn, too, with the Blackbird in an open quest for earthworms. Of the two species of spotty thrush commonly found in Britain, this is the one that loves small gardens. The Mistle Thrush prefers huge swards and wide open spaces.

Before the First World War the Song Thrush was commoner than the Blackbird, but ever since then their fortunes have diverged dramatically. The Blackbird until recently has been increasing, while the Song Thrush has been in long-term decline. Its numbers fell by fifty-three percent over twenty-five years up to 1999, and although figures released in 2003 showed a slight upturn, concerns are being raised about its long-term prospects for survival.

The problem is that we know about the recent decline, but we don't fully understand why it is happening. There have been dozens of suggestions, but none seems to carry the whole answer. Perhaps we shall never know; populations of birds are always subject to multiple pressures, with many forces equally able to tilt the fine ecological balance.

One of the most compelling reasons put forward for the decline has been the increase in the population of some of the Song Thrush's potential predators. Sparrowhawks take thrushes at all times of the year, and Magpies and Carrion Crows take eggs and young in the spring. All three have done well in recent years, at just the same time that the Song Thrush has been doing so badly. Some people take these bald facts as proof that the predators are the problem. But a closer look at the situation tends to erode the strength of their argument.

The most recent thorough study into the Song Thrush's fortunes has discovered an interesting dynamic at work. In most aspects of its life the Song Thrush is doing well. Adult birds are living, on average, just as long as they always have, and nesting success is unimpaired, too. The problem, it seems, lies with young adults in their first two or three months after fledging. Ironically, they are coming a cropper in large numbers just as they become old enough to be safe from the Magpies.

So what is the problem? Nobody knows for sure, but presumably the young birds are

With its arrow-shaped spots arranged in lines, the Song Thrush is distinguished from its larger relative, the Mistle Thrush.

A Song Thrush smashes open a snail shell. Each bird has special sites for this task, known as anvils.

not finding enough food. Britain has a less bird-friendly countryside than it used to, with hedgerows being grubbed up and with a reduction in the amount and quality of grassland. Herbicides have reduced the density of available food, and pesticides, too, have inhibited the richness of the environment.

Last-ditch Rations

One particular matter should be of special concern to gardeners. Song Thrushes are specialists on snails. These molluscs are not these birds' major food resource at most times of the year, but are a vital emergency food item in times when other nutriment becomes less available, such as dry summers and frozen winters. If we use too many molluscicides such as slug-pellets in our gardens, we might be adversely affecting the thrushes' supplies of last-ditch rations.

The link between pesticides and thrush numbers is not, however, proven, and the last three or four years have seen a welcome halt in the decline of this exceptional songster, especially in gardens. As yet, we do not fully understand what makes the Song Thrush prosper or suffer. If the story of the Song Thrush can teach us anything, it is that fluctuations in bird populations are very difficult to interpret. If a bird's decline can be seen as a crime, then perhaps we should treat it as a murder mystery. There are plenty of possible scenarios, plenty of false leads, and the prime suspect invariably turns out to be innocent.

MIDWINTER IS usually a curiously muted affair. With the days at their shortest, and the coldest season reaching its height, one might expect some spectacular show of force. There should be a huge storm, or days of snow or frost. But normally December is disappointingly dank and dismal, with short days of rain or fog, and interminable damp.

DECEMBER

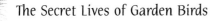

Winners and Losers

ALTHOUGH DECEMBER IS usually a quiet month meteorogically, there is nothing to stop the winter showing its teeth, and occasionally it does. When snowdrifts hit our shores in December, and stay for any length of time, they displace thousands of birds and kill many more. Ground-feeding species such as Skylarks and thrushes pour westwards and south-westwards in what are known as escape movements, migrating by day on and on until they see the ground beneath them turn green instead of white. In the garden, the residents suffer, dying in droves, too weak even to profit from bird tables. It is one of the few occasions when you can find dead birds, little frozen corpses kept refrigerated before the bugs and worms can reach them.

Even in those quiet Decembers, when small snow flurries cause raised eyebrows and conversation, the depopulation of birds is relentless. Day by day, birds succumb to all the usual hazards: predation, disease, starvation. They are ordinary birds with ordinary aptitudes, killed off by being ordinary. Winter's chill is not generous to such as these.

The Doomed Surplus

It's a cruel fact, but birds overproduce. Tits breed multitudes: from two parents may come ten eggs. Multiple-brooded Blackbirds and Robins are not far behind. By the end of the season they and their offspring are everywhere, each one a little bit of excess. Although many will travel and some will succumb in the early stages, there are still too many small bodies breathing each cubic metre of autumn air and getting fat on that season's own overproduction. They need winter to sort them out.

There is no room for anyone that isn't in first-rate condition. For not only is the winter a killer,

Previous Page: *Snow in December is cruel on the birds, but can bring unusual visitors to the garden (illustrated: Lapwings, Fieldfares, Redwings, Bramblings and Siskins, with Blackbird and Blue Tit)*

Right: *The presence of readily available food at feeders helps some less able birds survive. (Illustrated: Greenfinches, Great Tit and Blue Tits).*

so is competition. Resources are limited, and must be fought over. The ones that survive are winners, or even the winners among winners. The rest have been termed, by the most unsympathetic of scientific hearts, the 'doomed surplus'. They are the second-best: better than many, but below the elevated pass mark.

It's a sad thought at this seasonal time. As people we are hoping for happier things. Yet as we sleep in our beds, tucked up against the cold in our centrally heated bedrooms, we are also tucked up against the harsh realities of life outside our back door. Only yards from us, on a December night, the tame garden is wild and brutal.

But in our way, we ourselves can slightly upset that balance outside, tilting it in favour of the ordinary birds. By providing lots of regular food and water, we do help a few of the second-best to come through. We see something similar happening at city parks and squares, where unhealthy-looking pigeons with toes missing compete successfully with fitter individuals, helped by generous tourists throwing bread straight to them. The human heart can be an ecological factor.

It has been said by some that the bird table, with its food supplies available to strong and weak alike in this way, is producing a new, less genetically powerful strain of bird. By promoting the less fit, they say, we are diluting the quality of our visitors. All of a sudden, the doomed surplus isn't doomed any more, and it is not necessarily a good thing for the future. This is an argument borne of original and important thinking, and must be assembled into the picture of how bird feeding and bird husbandry will progress over the next decades. But how important a factor is it? Somehow the wild environment has a way of finding the weak out. If starvation doesn't get them, the other mainstays of bird culling probably will.

In the last twenty years wild birds have been welcomed into back gardens as never before, and bird feeding has sprouted an industry with considerable financial clout. There is less evidence that birds are weaker than before, and more that individuals are showing resourcefulness that we could never have predicted. The bird table and its accompanying fittings have, indeed,

become something of an ecological proving ground.

It is worth remembering too that, up until quite recently, there was no such thing as a garden bird at all and no such thing as a garden as we now know it. The tapestry of suburbia was only fashioned in the twentieth century, and bird feeding has only taken off as a major interest since the Second World War. The birds that we see in our gardens have not been there long. They are newcomers, still adapting to a constantly changing environment.

Space Invaders

The sight of a Robin on a spade might be a time-honoured icon to us, the very quintessence of December and the basis of a fortune in Christmas card sales. But Robins and spades are quite new acquaintances, and on the Continent the Robin is still a shy and wood-haunting species, avoiding people and sticking to the shade. Whenever you see one you should hum the National Anthem to yourself.

Gardens might be made for some species, such as Song Thrushes, birds that always lived in that interface between open ground and undergrowth that so much characterises gardens. But not all our characters have made such an easy transition. The Dunnock, at its roots, comes from mountain scrub. The Pied Wagtail preferred watery sites before it discovered lawns and roofs. Tits were woodland birds. House Martins and Swifts nested on cliffs or trees. All of these species have made pioneering movements, all of them in the comparatively recent past.

The Robin is an icon of the garden – but it wasn't always so, and it still isn't on the Continent.

The sight of Long-tailed Tits at a hanging nut feeder is a comparatively new one, only regular in the last ten years.

Perhaps the most impressive revolution has been undertaken by the Collared Dove. In the 1920s it languished over quite a wide range in the warm south-east of Europe and east to Asia, enjoying the company of human beings and their grain-filled farms and storehouses. It was a successful species with no reason to take the world by storm. Yet a few years later, presumably by dint of a genetic mutation, it suddenly underwent an expansion to its normal niche, making it tolerant of chillier, wetter climates. Within fifty years it had colonised most of western Europe, including Britain, and had become a fixture in our suburban gardens, taking the same kind of grain, and living in the same basic habitat.

The Magpie has not invaded countries, but it has, to much dismay, become a great deal commoner in our gardens over the last few decades. Despite prejudiced squeals to the contrary, this spread has not ridden on the back of the Magpie's occasional habit of munching up the young of our favourite song birds. It has just expanded its niche, as the Collared Dove has done. In particular, the Magpie has taken advantage of the growth of traffic in our towns and cities, and the consequent increase in small road casualties, which it fields in between oncoming cars. It also benefits from open turf, such as lawns and playing fields, where it obtains most of its food. And the sorts of trees that we often plant suit it rather well for nesting. We should really laud it for taking advantage of our way of life, although the Magpie seems to have done it all too easily, and that does not suit our country's mindset.

New Departures

It's not just the populations of birds that are changing; behaviour is, too. Take the Blackcap, for instance. Up until the 1960s this sweet-singing warbler was a common summer visitor to woods and large gardens, arriving in April and leaving by October, travelling down to the Mediterranean for a sun-kissed winter. But then it started being recorded in gardens out of season, and increasing numbers are now seen on British bird tables in winter. As yet, nobody is sure whether our breeding birds are staying behind or whether birds nesting farther north, for example in Scandinavia, are finishing their brief migrations here; recent evidence points to the latter. What is clear, however, is that the Blackcap's behaviour has altered as a result of their use of gardens.

It wasn't long ago, either, that the main visitors to hanging bird feeders were tits, sparrows and Greenfinches. Now all manner of other species are turning up, some of them from the most unlikely backgrounds. The Long-tailed Tit is a prime example. Despite its name it is not a true tit, and feeds on minute invertebrates, not nuts, throughout the winter season. In the last ten years, though, it is coming increasingly to hanging feeders stocked with peanuts and sunflower seeds. At first it was thought that these tentative visitors were seeking small insects attracted to the surface of the feeders. But no, the birds are taking fragments of nut, in a departure from their normal winter fare.

Robins, fed up with taking crumbs from feeding trays and on the ground, are also beginning to visit hanging feeders. They are not adapted to holding on to the mesh, so instead

Bramblings are unusual visitors to gardens, often appearing during bad weather.

they hover in front of the bag, pecking as they can, like ungainly hummingbirds. They have adapted this feeding technique from catching insects in the air, something they only occasionally do. It is another clear example of our garden birds' opportunism.

Amidst all this wonder and optimism, there are also birds whose stock appears to be falling. Twenty years ago we would be marvelling at the antics and intelligence of another garden bird, the House Sparrow, and being amazed at how it would learn to open milk bottles, peck shreds in crocuses or marigolds, nest down mine-shafts and come to be fed in the hand. But in recent years the House Sparrow has begun to decline sharply in some parts of the country. This drop in numbers has made headline news – especially since some of the greatest falls have been in urban London, where the journalists live and work! In fact the declines have been patchy, but the very idea that the House Sparrow could decrease at all would have been unthinkable a decade or two. It seemed like an ever-present, impregnable companion. Yet in some areas, the changing urban and suburban scene has clearly begun to work against it.

Another once abundant bird with apparently impregnable attachment to the garden is also declining: the Starling. This bird is possibly suffering from having fewer nest sites available, now that houses are being better maintained. It also has an anachronistic preference for untreated grassland, a disappearing commodity. It was never the most popular of birds, having the unfortunate tendency to come to the bird table in mugging gangs and to scatter all the adorable small birds away. It also has indelicate table manners, gulping its food down at a phenomenal and stomach-turning

rate, an adaptation to feeding quickly in dangerous situations. Yet its demise tells us important things about the garden scene, about whether they are beneficial or harmful, and whether they should be changed. We may never love it, but we must listen to what it tells us.

Bucking the Trend

Most birds are telling us good news and the Starling and House Sparrow are, for the moment, exceptions. This is just as well, too, because outside gardens in the wider landscape the picture for many birds is becoming rather bleak. On farmland, in particular, where efficient and ever-changing agricultural practice is shutting out birds, many once familiar species such as Skylarks and Yellowhammers are suffering sharp reductions in numbers. The same is happening in some other habitats, too. Gardens, it seems, are bucking the trend in that they are attracting ever more birds, of an increasing number of species.

Once upon a time, such an increase in garden birds would not be especially significant. But times have changed. As more and more people have become interested in birds in their gardens, so the amount of land under an ownership sympathetic to birds has increased dramatically, and is now enough to make a serious impact on populations as a whole. It's an oft-quoted fact that the area of gardens in Britain is greater than the extent of Britain's nature reserves, but it does prove that what we do in our gardens can really make a difference.

And so long as this is so, we will hopefully host more winners than losers.

The Holly and the Ivy – The Big Thrush's Story

THE STRAINS OF the Christmas carol The Holly and the Ivy are all too evident at this time of year: from churches, from street singers and from supermarket loudspeakers. It's hard to get away from them. Yet believe it or not, were it not for the unusual winter activities of a garden bird, the Mistle Thrush, the carol might never have been written.

The holly's fruits come out first in very late September, at a similar time to much other autumn produce. They quickly become popular with the local fruit-eaters, as many berry sources do. Blackbirds and Song Thrushes guzzle them eagerly in the early days and then, upon arriving in October, so do our winter visitors, the Redwings and Fieldfares. But then, almost overnight, the harvesting ceases. The berries stay on the trees, fresh and juicy and uneaten. It's as if they had somehow become poisoned by the colder air of the advancing autumn, and are now off everybody's shopping list.

But it's not like that at all. These holly berries are neither inedible nor shunned. In fact, it's quite the reverse. They are now appreciated and cherished to an obsessive degree. For pairs of Mistle Thrushes, they are the centre of the world.

Until the holly berries appear,

With its small head, heavy chest and big, round breast-spots, the Mistle Thrush can readily be distinguished from the smaller Song Thrush.

Mistle Thrushes spend the autumn travelling locally in informal, friendly flocks. But with the advent of the red fruits, these large thrushes become aloof and aggressive. Pairs stop wandering around, and settle in the vicinity of one or two favoured berry-bearing plants which,

with breathtaking cheek, they will gradually appropriate as their own private property. Nobody else will now be allowed close.

Bucking the Trend

This act of requisitioning, selfish though it is, makes perfect survival sense. With the berry supply firmly in their grip, Mistle Thrushes can make it their own personal winter larder. It's the perfect living food store, readily available as and when required. Holly berries are ideal for this type of husbandry, since they are long-lasting, resistant to frost, and will not all fall to the ground. What better way to ensure you have plenty to eat throughout the season?

Of course, the other birds in the area do not necessarily take kindly to this hogging of resources. But then the Mistle Thrush is the biggest of its family in Britain, with a heavy body and an ample chest like a beer gut. It will attack any suspiciously acting bird that comes near its living larder, driving it off even when it is a hundred metres (110 yd) away from the forbidden zone. After a few weeks of trying, most of the local berry-eaters recognise the futility of their attempts to trespass, and stay away.

What must really gall any onlookers is that, for much of the time, the Mistle Thrush guards don't actually use their resource at all. They simply spend their days foraging on the ground, never far away from their sacred trees, yet not plucking a single berry. To a hungry Blackbird or Redwing this must be torture to watch. To the owners, though, their actions are the height of expedience. They will forage terrestrially when the ground can deliver invertebrates that live in the soil. But if it's frosty or there's snow on the ground, only then they will they break into their precious supplies, and take what they need.

Occasionally the interlopers have the last laugh. When times are truly hard, outside flocks of hungry birds desperate for food become a pressure

A Mistle Thrush drives two Redwings away from a clump of mistletoe, another of its favoured food-plants.

that even the strongest Mistle Thrush cannot bear. Arriving in flocks, they are like a crowd overwhelming a small police presence. One bird can be attacked and driven off, but for every success there are a dozen failures as the trespassers stream in and feast upon the valuable fruit. Once overwhelmed, the Mistle Thrushes' food supply will be stripped within twenty-four hours. The owners give up and join in the feast, taking what they can, but without their conserved food supplies they will face an uncertain future.

In most winters, though, the Mistle Thrushes' store remains intact and it can last for a long time. There are many records of pairs keeping the holly bushes red until March, when they will relax their defence, and allow the berries to be taken by all comers. They might even feed berries from their once-defended trees to their early hatching young - prudent resource management, indeed.

Late in the season, especially if there is a cold snap, a Mistle Thrush may defend the first of the ivy berries instead as they come out in March,

rather than maintaining the holly's supply. And holly does not have a monopoly on the heart of this food-storing thrush. In some areas they will defend haws or branches of yew trees. And the name of the bird, of course, comes from its association with mistletoe. In many parts of the country, and especially on the Continent, mistletoe is the preferred option, with few other birds competing for the unusual white berries.

Christmas Decorations

However, in Britain, and especially in the garden environment, the Mistle Thrush is mostly a defender of hollies. Because of its defence, and its clever resource management, the holly berries still decorate the trees as Christmas approaches. If it were not for Mistle Thrushes, they would probably be gone before the festive season approached. Then, of course, the writer of the Christmas carol would have had to think of a different opening line.

Why Robins Don't Mind Christmas

WHAT MIGHT ROBINS be doing at this time of year, in between posing for Christmas cards or, less frivolously, in between doing their best to survive the harsh winter weather? The answer could surprise you.

Amazingly enough, they are pairing up – or at least, the early ones are. At this time when food stocks are low, the weather is a challenge and spring must seem a world away, some Robins are finding it within themselves to devote a little time to the delicate art of courtship.

Robins, you will remember, have for some months been in a state that could be called Red Alert. During the autumn and early winter they have been in territorial mood, aggressively evicting each other from their respective territories, and keeping well apart. Both sexes have been singing insults to all corners, demanding that everyone keeps off their hallowed patch of ground. No one wants to concede any ground.

But sometime in the middle of this last month of the year, a male Robin in spring-like mood takes it upon himself to suddenly change his tune. His autumn songs have been mellow and moody, and sung from a low perch, almost out of sight.

But now, just for a few days, he abruptly changes key. The singer sings more often, more openly, and with shorter, more cheerful-sounding phrases. He adheres more to the centre of his territory than he has done before, and he climbs up higher to deliver his phrases.

That's not to say that his mood has improved. He might be singing his pairing song, but that doesn't mean he will recognise, or even welcome any approach from a female. He needs to be won over.

Robins are good at sex equality, and it tends to be the female that takes the initiative in pairing. It's the Robin way. A female hears the right sort of song, and then it's up to her to go and meet the singer. At first she makes short incursions into a territory, and is almost always rapidly and physically rebuffed by the owner. A less determined bird would be put off by such rough treatment, but not a female Robin. She would expect nothing less.

Song and Following

It might take quite a few visits from a prospective mate before the owner twigs that he is the object of welcome interest. Once he does so, though, he becomes highly excited. He hops down to the ground in response to her 'tick' calls, and sings loudly not far in front of her. This triggers a delightful display known as the 'song-and-following ceremony'. The male sings and the female approaches; the male sings again and the female approaches again. As if intimidated, the male pecks at the ground. Once again he sings and once again she follows. Then, in a sudden fit of zest, the female chases the male round and round his territory, the two birds hopping and flying and, during brief pauses, singing as if both had a fit of the giggles. Their antics cease only when the female abruptly leaves the territory. The male does not want to stop the fun, and so he follows the female on to another's territory. He is taking a risk; the male next door is unlikely to be sharing his joie de vivre, and will violently evict him. More often, the male stays put, hoping for a next time.

The familiar Robin has a Christmas secret.

A female can make several visits to several males during the month and treat them all in much the same way, but eventually she must and will decide on her choice of future mate. A sure sign of two recently paired Robins in December is to see them foraging side by side on the lawn, treating each other with that air of calm detachment that often speaks of comfort.

Curiously, this is very much a midwinter fling. The male will soon revert to singing from more concealed perches, as he did before, although he will no longer sing his autumn song. The female might even return to her territory, if she has one, or amalgamate hers with his; it depends on where she started. But neither sex shows much obvious affection to the other, and there are few outward signs that they are a pair until they begin to breed several months later. It's tempting to call this an 'engagement period', but one without rings or rituals. But it's certainly binding, and neither sex will suddenly change partner in the interim.

But Robins, you see, don't mind Christmas. A little bit of pair bonding behaviour must give them welcome relief during the long, hard winter.

Mob Rule

FROM TIME TO time, a small bird comes across an owl at its roost site. One might expect that, upon discovering such a lethal predator at alarmingly close quarters, it would flee as far away as possible, relieved to escape with its life. But this isn't what most birds do. Instead, they enter into the curious ritual known as 'mobbing'. The finder calls loudly to summon other birds to the scene, and within minutes a dozen or more individuals of several different species will be also be calling with all their might, and making occasional excursions closer to the predator to have a better look.

Mobbing is an exciting phenomenon to see in the garden. If you hear a Blackbird giving its 'chink, chink' call in the middle of the day, it's often a sign that something is afoot. The Blackbirds – and there are often several - fly in agitation from perch to perch, adding in long, rattling alarm calls. Approach carefully and you might well observe and hear other species nearby – Robins, for example, giving 'tick, tick' calls and Wrens going 'teck, teck'. The former curtsey crossly, the latter cock their tails and flick their wings. Great Tits scold, Chaffinches go 'pink, pink'. An air of intense excitement pervades the scene.

With all this unwelcome attention, one might expect that the owl would become both confused and very angry. The loud, high-pitched calls must assault its sensitive ears, and its instinct, one would imagine, would be to lash out at its tormentors. But despite the fact that, very occasionally, a mobbing bird ends up in the talons of its target, the owl is essentially powerless to resist. The smaller birds are very alert and highly adept at dodging back and forth. An owl, like many a bird of prey, is a master of the art of surprise. Without this weapon, it is impotent.

Outnumbered and Irritated

After a few minutes of a mobbing, the final act is inevitable. The owl, outnumbered and irritated, takes a flight into the bright daylight and spirits itself away. Gradually the successful mobbers melt back to their day jobs, giving the occasional call in triumph, and they focus attention once again on their most important task of the day, foraging.

The question is: why do they do it? Mobbing is an activity fraught with risk. There is a chance that it could all go wrong, with bloodshed and casualties, and it is also energetically consuming, a drain on generally scarce resources.

The most obvious answer is that mobbing confuses an enemy, annoys it and moves it on. Birds are not machines; a daytime disturbance could theoretically impair an owl's hunting performance later at night. And, by shifting an owl from its roost a bird could be seeing it away from its own territory, and away from its family, nest or eggs. The enemy's physical presence is removed, to obvious benefit in the future. If so, mobbing could be deemed a priority activity, even in times of hardship.

Mobbing could also, at least temporarily, persuade the owl that a certain bird is far too fit, agile and alert to catch. It seems highly unlikely that any predator will remember the face of its tormentor, and recognise it in the future as one that is not worth chasing. But the owl might possibly be persuaded that the birds in a certain area are a rowdy crowd, well worth leaving alone.

One of the most interesting suggestions about mobbing is that it is an educational activity. There is no particular reason that a young bird should know exactly what every predator looks like, although some predator recognition is instinctive. Perhaps attending a mobbing is a way of finding out? Perhaps birds take their fledglings to an owl and point it out as dangerous, much as we might take a child aside and warn it against the dangers of talking to strangers? More likely, birds from a wide area might be attracted to the commotion, and learn of their own accord. It is an interesting theory, and has some credence.

It's not only owls that are mobbed. Any potentially dangerous animal may be subject to such unwelcome attention, from a Sparrowhawk to a cat. Some birds are mobbed in flight, some only on perches. It's a widespread, year-round activity. Some time, in your garden, you are bound to see it happening, and then you can muse on the reasons behind this dangerous and high-octane enterprise for yourself.

A Tawny Owl and its band of persecutors: (clockwise from bottom) Wren, Chaffinch, Great Tit, Blue Tit, and Great Tit again.

Epilogue

AND SO, in December, the human year comes to an end. The last few days between Christmas and January 1st often seem to peter out as we wait for the new start, with its resolutions and promise. Yet the birds are already getting ready for their year. December holds the shortest day, and sees the first shifts towards breeding, even in the damp and dark. December isn't the end, it's the beginning.

Inquiring minds are also on a never-ending loop. Every year – perhaps every month – sees a new discovery, large or small, about our garden birds. This cycle of enquiry will continue to throw up new things so long as we watch and care about the feathered creatures that share our space. Recently, for example, it has been discovered that Starlings use their previously unheralded sense of smell to select the correct nest material. And crows have been demonstrating their intelligence in ways we could scarcely have imagined. Many nourishing morsels of knowledge await around the corner, and they always will.

Some questions, though, continue year after year to elude us. We are still unclear about many aspects of migration, of how birds find their way and know when they've arrived. And we don't even know, for certain, why the humble wagtail actually wags its tail, or why Siskins always seem to hang upside down to feed. But that's good. Even as the year turns, at least some aspects of the lives of our garden birds can remain, for a while longer, a secret.

Bibliography

Berthold, P. 2001. *Bird Migration: A General Survey*. (2nd edition). Oxford University Press.

Brooke, M. and Birkhead, T. (eds) 1991. *The Cambridge Encyclopedia of Ornithology*. Cambridge University Press.

Burton, R. 1990. *Birdfeeder Handbook*. Dorling Kindersley.

Cannon, A. 1998. *Garden BirdWatch Handbook*. 2nd edition. British Trust for Ornithology.

Catchpole, C.K. and Slater, P.J.B. 1995. *Bird Song: Biological Themes and Variations*. Cambridge University Press.

Cramp, S. and Simmons, K.E.L. (eds.) 1977-83. *Handbook of the Birds of Europe, the Middle East and North Africa: The Birds of the Western Palearctic, Vols 1-3*. Oxford University Press.

Cramp, S. (ed.) 1985-92. *Handbook of the Birds of Europe, the Middle East and North Africa: The Birds of the Western Palearctic, Vols 4-6*. Oxford University Press.

Cramp, S. and Perrins, C.M. (eds.) 1993-94. *Handbook of the Birds of Europe, the Middle East and North Africa: The Birds of the Western Palearctic, Vols 7-9*. Oxford University Press.

Davies, N.R. 1990. Dunnocks: Cooperation and conflict among males and females in a variable mating system. In Stacey, P.B. and Koenig, W.D. (eds.) *Cooperative Breeding in Birds*. Cambridge University Press.

Del Hoyo, J., Elliott, A. and Sargatal, J. (eds.) 1992- *Handbook of Birds of the World, Vols 1-7*. Lynx Edicions.

Ehrlich, P.R., Dobkin, D.S., Wheye, D. and Pimm, S.L. 1994. *The Birdwatcher's Handbook*. Oxford University Press.

Gibbons, D.W., Reid, J.B. and Chapman, R.A. 1993. *The New Atlas of Breeding Birds in Britain and Ireland: 1988-1991*. T & AD Poyser.

Gibbons, Bob & Liz. 1988. *Creating a Wildlife Garden*. Hamlyn.

Holden, P. and Cleeves, T. 2002. *RSPB Handbook of British Birds*. Christopher Helm.

Lack, P. (ed.) 1986. *The Atlas of Wintering Birds in Britain and Ireland*. T & AD Poyser.

Mead, C. 2000. *The State of the Nation's Birds*. Whittet Books.

Newton, I. 1972. *Finches*. New Naturalist Series. Collins.

Perrins, C. 1979. *British Tits*. New Naturalist Series. Collins.

Perrins, C. 1987. *Collins New Generation Guide: Birds of Britain and Europe*. Collins.

Snow, B. and Snow, D. 1988. *Birds and Berries*. T & AD Poyser.

Soper, T. 1992. *The Bird Table Book* (6th ed). David & Charles.

Turner, A.K. 1994. *The Swallow*. Hamlyn.

Wernham, C.V., Toms, M.P., Marchant, J.H., Clark, J.A., Siriwardena, G.M. and Baillie, S.R. (eds.) 2002. *The Migration Atlas: Movements of the Birds of Britain and Ireland*. T & AD Poyser.

Witherby, H.F., Jourdain, F.C.R., Ticehurst, N.F. and Tucker, B.W. 1938-41. *The Handbook of British Birds, Vols 1-5*. HF & G Witherby.

Acknowledgements

This book began as a lecture, designed to while away evenings for various bird clubs and RSPB groups – so my thanks are due to those who made positive comments about the talk. Thanks, too, to my wife Carolyn for pointing out that the one could be transformed into the other – this book was really her idea.

Many thanks to Nigel Redman at A&C Black for being willing to make the idea a reality, to Paula McCann for her design skills and to Sylvia Sullivan and Marianne Taylor for their editorial expertise.

And special thanks to my editor, Mike Unwin, for all his hard work in seeing the project through from start to finish. Nigel – give the man a pay rise.

Big thanks to Peter Partington for his fantastic artwork – we knew he was just the right man for the job. And special thanks to Gordon Langsbury for both his photographs and his infectious enthusiasm.

Finally, thanks are due to the many patient and curious researchers who, by always asking questions, actually provided all the material for this book, and uncovered the secret lives of garden birds.

Index

Page numbers in **bold** refer to illustrations